A-Z EXETER

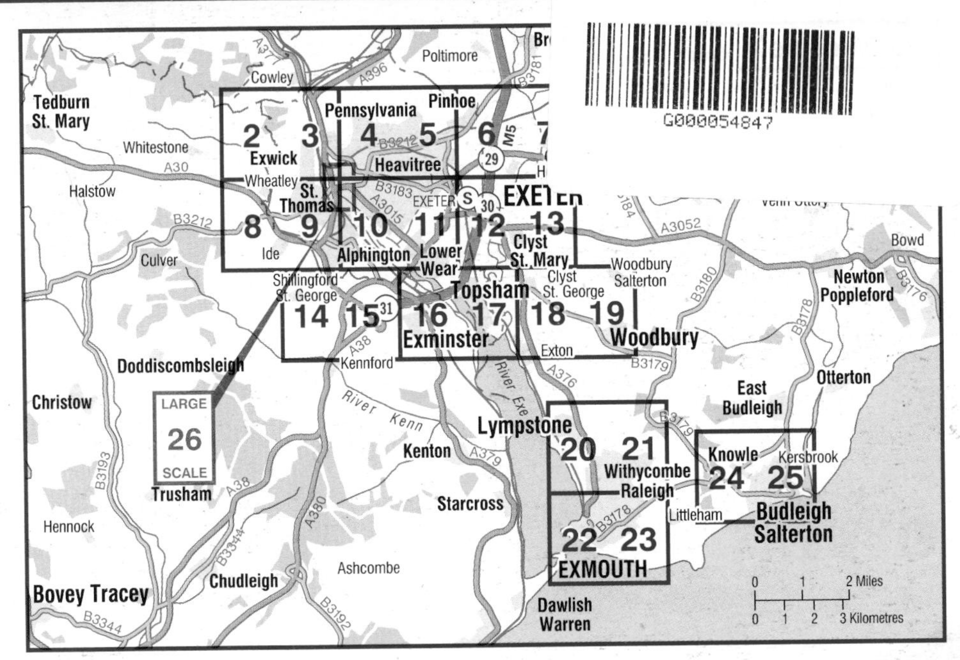

Reference

Motorway	M5
A Road	A30
Under Construction	
B Road	B3212
Dual Carriageway	
One Way Street Traffic flow on A roads is indicated by a heavy line on the drivers' left.	
Pedestrianized Road	
Restricted Access	
Track & Footpath	
Residential Walkway	
Railway	Level Crossing / Station

Built Up Area	MILL LA.
Local Authority Boundary	
Postcode Boundary	
Map Continuation	5 / 26
Car Park Selected	P
Church or Chapel	†
Cycle Route Selected	
Fire Station	
Hospital	H
House Numbers A & B Roads only	27 / 8
Information Centre	i
National Grid Reference	293

Police Station	▲
Post Office	★
Toilet with facilities for the Disabled	
Educational Establishment	
Hospital or Health Centre	
Industrial Building	
Leisure or Recreational Facility	
Place of Interest	
Public Building	
Shopping Centre or Market	
Other Selected Buildings	

Scale 4 inches (10.16cm) to 1 mile
1:15,840 6.31cm to 1 km

0 ¼ ½ Mile
0 250 500 750 Metres 1 Kilometre

Geographers' A-Z Map Company Ltd.

Head Office: Fairfield Road, Borough Green, Sevenoaks, Kent TN15 8PP Tel: 01732 781000 (General Enquiries & Trade Sales)
Showrooms: 44 Gray's Inn Road, London WC1X 8HX Tel: 020 7440 9500 (Retail Sales)
www.a-zmaps.co.uk

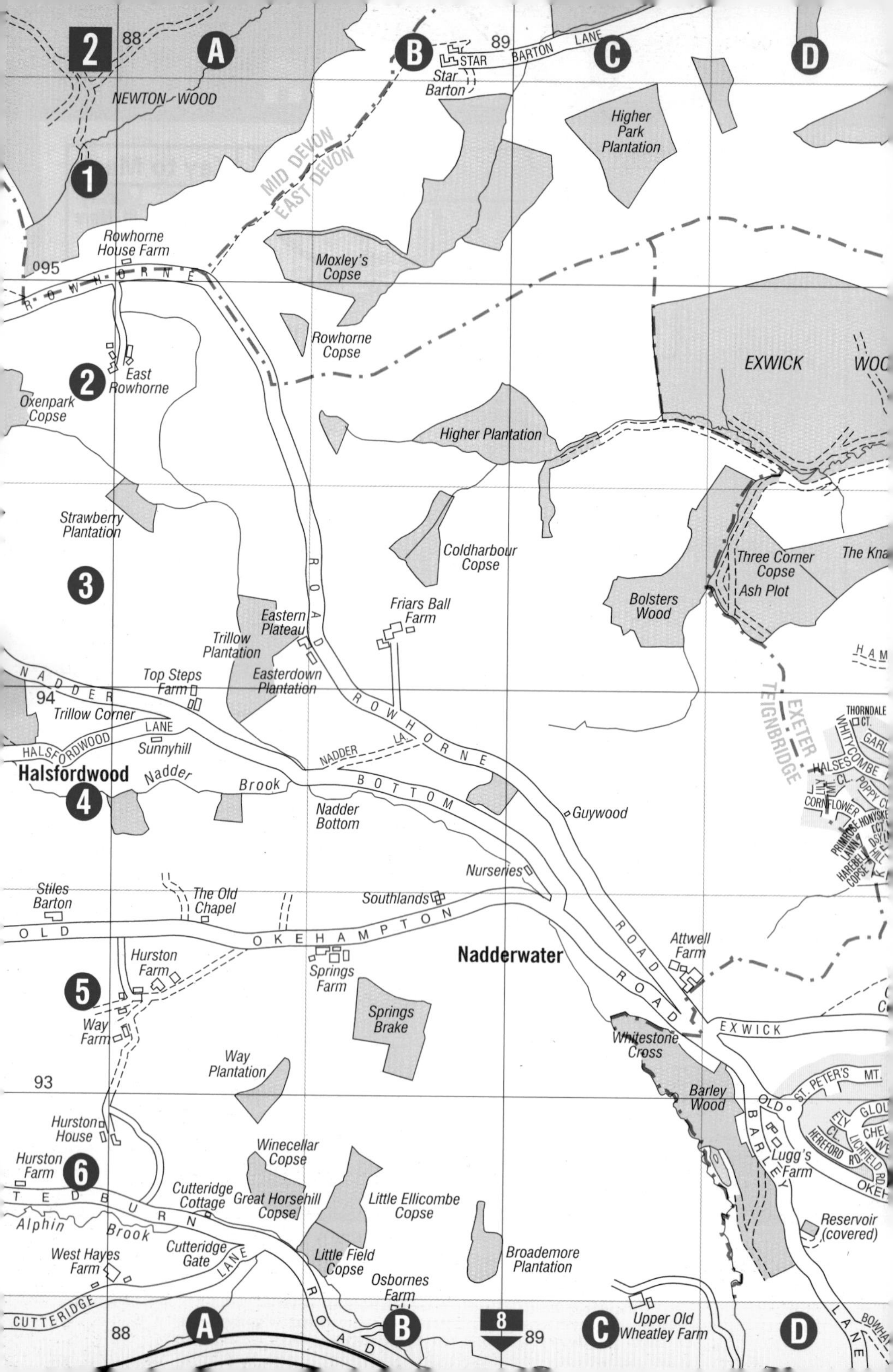
2
88
A
B
89
C
D
STAR BARTON LANE
Star Barton
NEWTON WOOD
Higher Park Plantation
MID DEVON
EAST DEVON
1
Rowhorne House Farm
095
ROWHORNE
Moxley's Copse
Rowhorne Copse
EXWICK WOO
East Rowhorne
2
Oxenpark Copse
Higher Plantation
Strawberry Plantation
Coldharbour Copse
Three Corner Copse
The Kna
Ash Plot
3
Bolsters Wood
Friars Ball Farm
Eastern Plateau
Trillow Plantation
Easterdown Plantation
ROAD
Top Steps Farm
NADDER
94
Trillow Corner
LANE
HALSFORDWOOD
Sunnyhill
Halsfordwood
Nadder Brook
NADDER LA.
ROWHORNE
BOTTOM
4
Nadder Bottom
Guywood
EXETER
TEIGNBRIDGE
THORNDALE CT.
WHITYCOMBE
HALSES
CORNFLOWER
Nurseries
Stiles Barton
The Old Chapel
Southlands
OLD OKEHAMPTON
Hurston Farm
Springs Farm
Nadderwater
Attwell Farm
5
ROAD
Springs Brake
Way Farm
EXWICK
Whitestone Cross
Way Plantation
93
Barley Wood
ST. PETER'S MT.
OLD BARLEY
Hurston House
Winecellar Copse
HEREFORD RD.
LICHFIELD RD.
Lugg's Farm
Hurston Farm
6
Cutteridge Cottage
Great Horsehill Copse
Little Ellicombe Copse
TEDBURN
Alphin Brook
Reservoir (covered)
Cutteridge Gate
Little Field Copse
Broademore Plantation
West Hayes Farm
LANE
Osbornes Farm
CUTTERIDGE
ROAD
Upper Old Wheatley Farm
88
A
B
8
89
C
D
LANE
BOWHAY

3
92
E
F
G
H
Cowley
Sewage Works
CREDITON RD. A377
STOKE A396 RD.
Barton Place Wood
Barton Place (Hostel)
Barton Place Farm
Hidden Valley
Cowley Bridge
ST. ANDREW'S RD.
WREFORD'S LA.
WREFORD'S DR.
WREFORD'S LANE
GREENACRES
Bellenden
1
BELLE VUE RD.
Bellevue Farm
Rose Cottage
Pennsylvania Picnic S.
EAST DEVON
EXETER
Exwick Weir
COWLEY
RIDGEWAY
GARTH
ROUNDHILL CL.
CHERRY TREE
WOODLEIGH CL.
ALLINGTON MEAD
BELLE VUE
Cottage Farm
095
WEST
Play. Fld.
ARGYLL ROAD
Thomas Hall
GT. DURYARD COTTS.
Argyll Gdns.
Sundown Gardens
Exwick Barton
Creedy
RIVER EXE
River
2
Weirs
The Cottage
The Oaks
Duryard Halls of Residence
Duryard
Duryard Grange
BELVIDERE
Higher Hoopern Farm
Reservoir (covered)
Eco. Lab
Exwick Leat
BRIDGE
LWR. ARGYLL RD.
COPPLESTONE DR.
HIGH CROFT
Grassway Wood
Playing Field
UNIVERSITY OF EXETER (STREATHAM CAMPUS)
RENNES DR.
Halwill
GLENTHORNE RD.
CLYDESDALE
GRAFTON RD.
Sports Hall
3
KING EDWARD ST.
GRAFTON
EX4
Birks Halls of Residence
Mardon Hall
MARDON HILL
STOCKER
NORTH PARK RD.
Amory Building
Weirs
Northcott Theatre
Shop. Cen.
4
94
A377
Exwick Mills
Reed Hall
THE QUEEN'S DRIVE
Great Hall
PRINCE OF WALES RD.
Hatherly Lab.
LANE
HILL
ROAD
NEW ROAD
LODGE HILL
STREATHAM
FESTIVE RD.
Lib.
Pav.
Devon County Cricket Grd.
RUSHFORTH PL.
LIFFEY RISE
GUINNESS LA.
FARM WAY
IVEAGH CT.
RIVERVIEW DR.
EXWICK CT.
KILBARRAN RI.
HAREFIELD CL.
Knightley
PERRY RD.
KINGSWOOD CL.
KINNERTON CT.
RACKFIELD COTTS.
EXE VW. COTTS.
TADDIFORDE CT. MANS.
Red Cow Village
PRINCE
HOWARD CL.
MOORLAND
STATION RD.
WAGGONERS WAY
RED COW VILLAGE
STREATHAM RISE
Brook
Hoopern Valley
Taddiforde
St. David's
Exwick
BURRATOR DR.
HAYTOR DR.
DRIVE
EXWICK HILL
TADDYFORDE CT.
TADDIFORDE RD.
ELMBROOK
THORNLEA
Higher Barracks
Exeter St. Davids
WINDSOR CL.
HOWELL RD.
B3183
ELWELL
LINDEN VALE
EXWICK
Exwick Mid. Sch.
PALMERSTON DR.
VALLEY RD.
OLD BAKERY CL.
OLD'S VIEW
BONHAY
ST. CLEMENTS LA.
ATTWILL'S ALMSHOUSES
Exeter College
Bury Mdw.
ELM GRO.
H.M. Prison Remand Home
5
Cleve House
KNOWLE
GLOUCESTER
Foxhayes First Sch.
FAIRHAZEL DR.
ROWAN
NEW VALLEY
TELFORD RD.
NORTH
WOODBINE
BLACKALL ROAD
PINE AV.
Exwick Play. Flds.
TAVISTOCK RD.
HELE RD.
Clock Tower
CANTERBURY ROAD
TRURO DR.
CYPRESS DR.
LOOE RD.
Offices
Exeter Central
Northernhay Gdns.
CHESTER CL.
PETERBOROUGH RD.
WINCHESTER
MILDMAY CL.
SIMEY CL.
QUEEN ST.
93
Crown Ct.
Castle
GUILDFORD CL.
EDINBURGH
LINCOLN
NORWICH RD.
COVENTRY RD.
CLEVE RD.
ENNERDALE WY.
Playing Fields
Ten. Cts.
Sports Ground
RIVER EXE
PEEP LA.
RUSSELL
RICHMOND RD.
STATION
Sch.
26
Coll.
Univ. Mus.
Dis. Cen.
Lib.
Foxhayes
ST. ALBANS CL.
Exwick Cemetery
GUYS ROAD
EXETER
Comm. Cen.
LWR. NTH. ST.
IRON BRI.
NORTHERNHAY ST.
ST. PAUL ST.
QUEEN ST.
MUSGRAVE
ADDISON CLOSE
HADRIAN DR.
ANTONINE
ROAD
Exe Valley
Mount Dinham
ROCKSIDE VS.
Weir
Exeter Coll.
DINHAM CRES.
DINHAM RD.
BELL CT.
CEMETERY PL.
SHOP. CEN.
6
ASHLEIGH MT. RD.
ASHLEIGH CL.
Sch.
WINDERMERE CL.
LAKELANDS DR.
Weir Way
Weir
A377 ROAD
STREET
NORTH ST.
MARY ARCHES ST.
HIGH ST.
CATHEDRAL YD.
CATH.
CLOISTERS
The Close
Redhills
REDHILLS CL.
HIGHER BARLEY MT.
WELLPARK CL.
LANDHAYS RD.
Play. Fld.
EAGLE COTTS.
BARTHOLOMEW ST. E.
SOUTH ST.
Hall
Sch.
9
91
WESTERN WY.
290

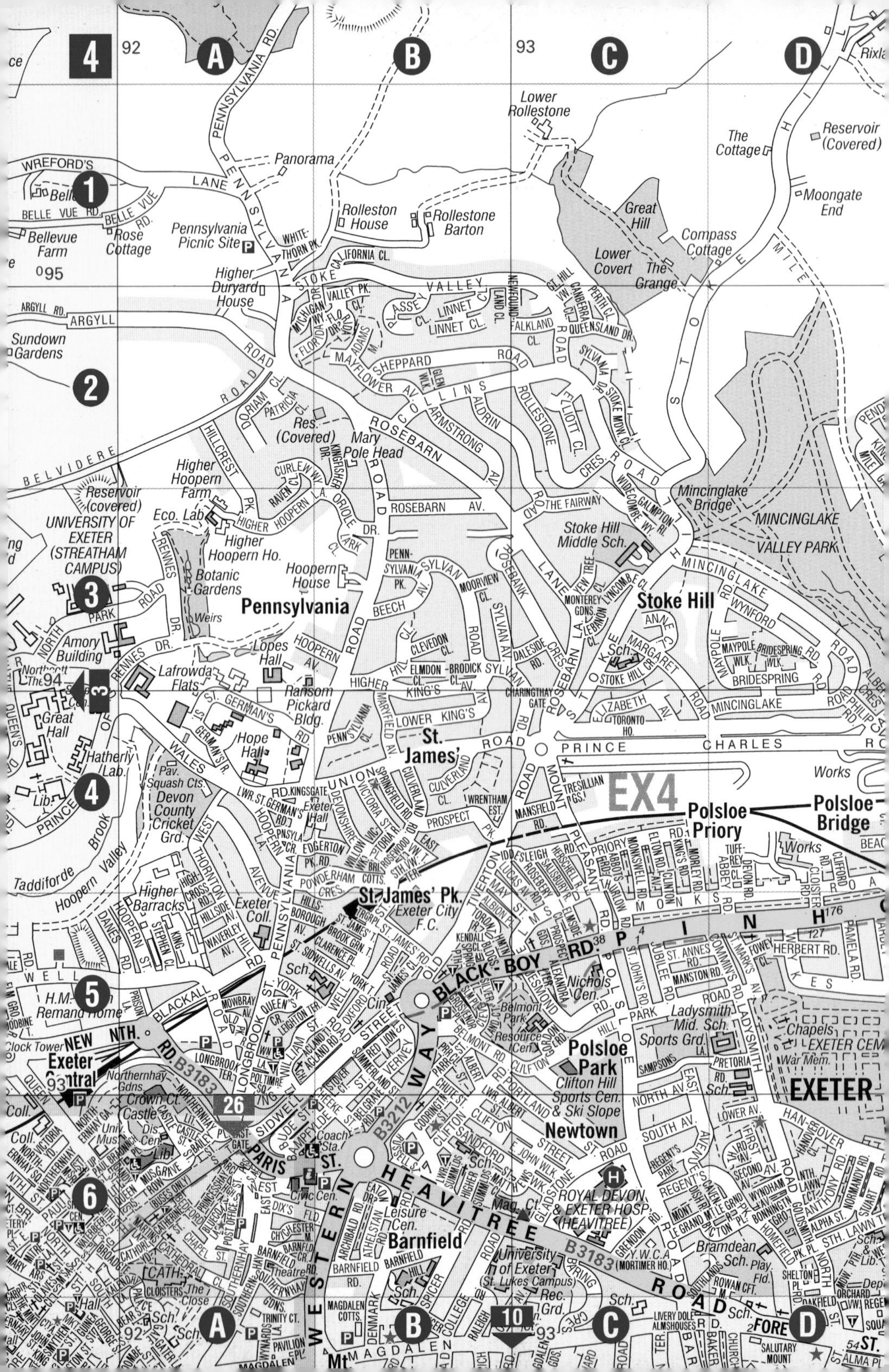
4
92
93
A
B
C
D
Pennsylvania
Stoke Hill
St. James'
EX4
Polsloe Priory
Polsloe Bridge
Polsloe Park
Newtown
Barnfield
EXETER
Lower Rollestone
Panorama
Rolleston House
Rollestone Barton
Pennsylvania Picnic Site
Higher Duryard House
Bellevue Farm
Rose Cottage
Sundown Gardens
Great Hill
Lower Covert
The Grange
Compass Cottage
The Cottage
Reservoir (Covered)
Moongate End
Res. (Covered)
Mary Pole Head
Higher Hoopern Farm
Reservoir (covered)
UNIVERSITY OF EXETER (STREATHAM CAMPUS)
Eco. Lab
Higher Hoopern Ho.
Hoopern House
Botanic Gardens
Weirs
Amory Building
Lopes Hall
Lafrowda Flats
Ransom Pickard Bldg.
Great Hall
Hope Hall
Hatherly Lab.
Lib.
Pav.
Squash Cts.
Devon County Cricket Grd.
Exeter Hall
Mincinglake Bridge
MINCINGLAKE VALLEY PARK
Stoke Hill Middle Sch.
Works
Higher Barracks
Exeter Coll.
St. James' Pk.
Exeter City F.C.
H.M. Remand Home
Clock Tower
Exeter Central
Northernhay Gdns.
Crown Ct.
Castle
Univ. Mus.
Dis. Cen.
Lib.
Nichols Cen.
Belmont Park
Resource Cen.
Clifton Hill Sports Cen. & Ski Slope
Ladysmith Mid. Sch.
Sports Grd.
Chapels
EXETER CEM
War Mem.
ROYAL DEVON & EXETER HOSP. (HEAVITREE)
Coach Sta.
Civic Cen.
Leisure Cen.
University of Exeter (St. Lukes Campus)
Rec. Grd.
Y.W.C.A. (MORTIMER HO.)
Bramdean Sch.
Play Fld.
LIVERY DOLE ALMSHOUSES
SALUTARY MOUNT
The Close
Theatre
Hall
CATH.
CATHEDRAL
CLOISTERS
PENNSYLVANIA RD.
LANE
BELLE VUE RD.
WREFORD'S
ARGYLL RD.
ROAD
BELVIDERE
STOKE VALLEY
WHITE-THORN PK.
CALIFORNIA CL.
MICHIGAN WY.
FLORIDA DR.
PLASSEY CL.
LINNET CL.
NEWFOUNDLAND CL.
FALKLAND CL.
CANBERRA CL.
QUEENSLAND DR.
PERTH CL.
MAYFLOWER AV.
SHEPPARD ROAD
COLLINS
ROSEBARN
ARMSTRONG AV.
ALDRIN
ROLLESTONE CRES.
ELLIOTT CL.
STOKE MDW. CL.
STOKE HILL
HILLCREST PK.
DORIAM CL.
PATRICIA
CURLEW WY.
RAVEN CL.
KINGFISHER DR.
ORIOLE DR.
LARK CL.
HIGHER HOOPERN LA.
ROSEBARN AV.
THE FAIRWAY
WIDECOMBE WY.
GALMPTON RI.
MINCINGLAKE RD.
WYNFORD RD.
RENNES DR.
NORTH PARK ROAD
PENNSYLVANIA ROAD
SYLVAN AV.
MOORVIEW CL.
ROSEBANK CRES.
BEECH AV.
HOOPERN AV.
CLEVEDON CL.
ELMDON CL.
BRODICK CL.
HIGHER KING'S AV.
LOWER KING'S AV.
DALESIDE RD.
ROSEBARN LA.
MARGARET RD.
STOKE HILL CR.
ELIZABETH AV.
TORONTO HO.
MAYPOLE WLK.
BRIDESPRING WLK.
BRIDESPRING RD.
CHARINGTHAY GATE
PRINCE CHARLES ROAD
ST. GERMAN'S RD.
WALES
CULVERLAND CL.
WRENTHAM EST.
PROSPECT PK.
MOUNT PLEASANT RD.
TRESILLIAN GDS.
MANSFIELD RD.
UNION RD.
DEVONSHIRE PL.
VICTORIA ST.
SPRINGFIELD RD.
HOOPERN LA.
WEST AVENUE
THORNTON HILL
EDGERTON PK. RD.
POWDERHAM CRES.
PRIORY RD.
MONKS ROAD
PINHOE
BLACK - BOY RD.
POLSLOE RD.
ST. JOHN'S RD.
JUBILEE RD.
ST. ANNES RD.
MANSTON RD.
HERBERT RD.
PAMELA RD.
BLACKALL ROAD
NEW NTH. RD.
B3183
LONGBROOK ST.
QUEEN'S CR.
YORK RD.
OXFORD RD.
WESTERN WAY
B3212
HEAVITREE ROAD
PARIS ST.
SIDWELL ST.
BELMONT RD.
PORTLAND ST.
CLIFTON RD.
SANDFORD ST.
GLADSTONE RD.
NORTH AV.
SOUTH AV.
REGENT'S PARK
HANOVER ROAD
FORE ST.
MAGDALEN
Hoopern Valley
Taddiforde Brook
WELL ST.
DANES RD.
PRISON LA.
26
10
3
94
95
93
92
Sch.

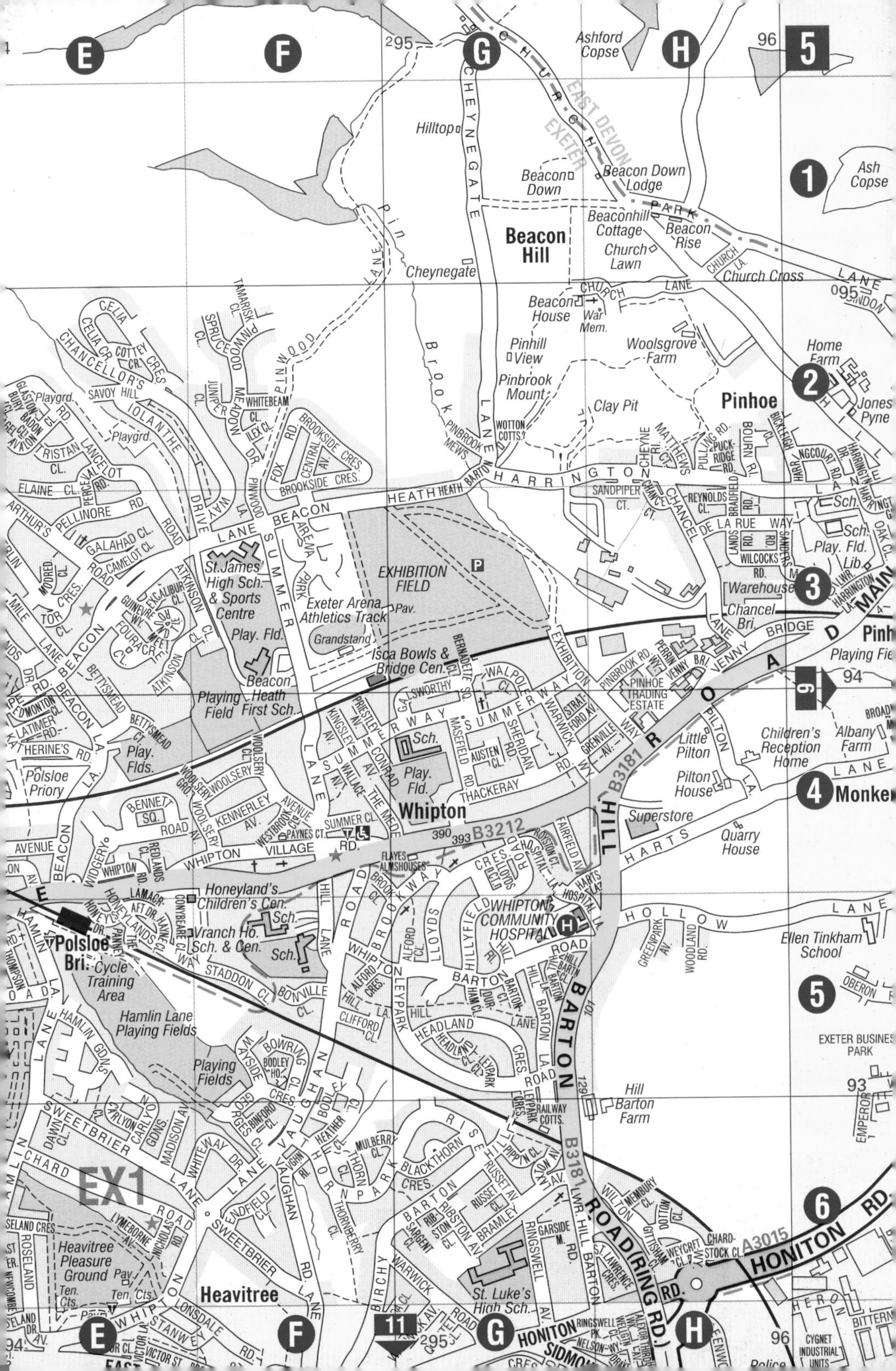

5
E
F
G
H
295
96
Ashford Copse
Ash Copse
Hilltop
Beacon Down
Beacon Down Lodge
EAST DEVON
EXETER
CHURCH HILL
PARK LANE
Beaconhill Cottage
Beacon Rise
Beacon Hill
Church Lawn
Church Cross
CHURCH LA.
CHURCH LANE
Cheynegate
CHEYNEGATE
Beacon House
War Mem.
Pinhill View
Woolsgrove Farm
Home Farm
Pinbrook Mount
Clay Pit
Pinhoe
Jones Pyne
PINBROOK MEWS
WOTTON COTTS.
HARRINGTON LANE
HEATH BARTON
BROOKSIDE CRES.
CENTRAL AV.
FOX RD.
PINWOOD LA.
PINWOOD MEADOW DR.
WHITEBEAM CL.
ILEX CL.
JUNIPER CL.
SPRUCE CL.
TAMARISK CL.
CELIA CR.
COTTEY CRES.
CHANCELLOR'S WAY
SAVOY HILL
IOLANTHE DRIVE
Playgrd.
LANCELOT RD.
ELAINE CL.
PELLINORE RD.
ARTHUR'S ROAD
GALAHAD CL.
CAMELOT CL.
BEACON LANE
SUMMER LANE
ARENA PARK
EXHIBITION FIELD
Exeter Arena Athletics Track
Pav.
Grandstand
St. James' High Sch. & Sports Centre
Play. Fld.
Beacon Heath First Sch.
Playing Field
Isca Bowls & Bridge Cen.
EXHIBITION WAY
SANDPIPER CT.
CHANCEL LANE
REYNOLDS CL.
DE LA RUE WAY
WILCOCKS RD.
Warehouse
Chancel Bri.
Sch.
Play. Fld.
Lib.
VENNY BRIDGE
MAIN ROAD
Pinhoe
Playing Field
94
PINHOE TRADING ESTATE
PINBROOK RD.
B3181
Little Pilton
Pilton House
PILTON LA.
Children's Reception Home
Albany Farm
Monkerton
LANE
WALPOLE CL.
SUMMER WAY
GALSWORTHY
KINGSLEY AV.
PRIESTLEY AV.
CONRAD AV.
MASEFIELD RD.
AUSTEN CL.
SHERIDAN RD.
WARWICK WAY
GRENVILLE AV.
THACKERAY RD.
THE MEDE
Whipton
Sch.
Play. Fld.
Superstore
HARTS LANE
Quarry House
B3212
390
393
WHIPTON VILLAGE RD.
SUMMER CL.
PAYNES CT.
FLAYES ALMSHOUSES
BROOK WAY
ROSTON CT.
FAIRFIELD AV.
HOSPITAL LA.
WHIPTON COMMUNITY HOSPITAL
HOLLOW LANE
GREENPARK AV.
WOODLAND RD.
Ellen Tinkham School
OBERON RD.
EXETER BUSINESS PARK
93
EMPEROR WAY
BETTYSMEAD
Polsloe Priory
WOOLSERY AV.
KENNERLEY AV.
BENNETT SQ.
AVENUE
BEACON AV.
WIDGERY RD.
WHIPTON RD.
REDLANDS CL.
Honeyland's Children's Cen.
Sch.
Vranch Ho. Sch. & Cen.
Polsloe Bri.
Cycle Training Area
Hamlin Lane Playing Fields
STADDON CL.
BONVILLE CL.
WHIPTON LA.
HILL LANE
LLOYDS CRES.
ALFORD CRES.
HILLYFIELD RD.
BARTON ROAD
HILL BARTON LA.
LEYPARK RD.
HEADLAND CRES.
CLIFFORD CL.
Playing Fields
BOWRING CL.
BODLEY CL.
VAUGHAN RD.
HEATHER CL.
MULBERRY CL.
BLACKTHORN CRES.
THORN PARK RISE
HILL BARTON
129
Hill Barton Farm
RAILWAY COTTS.
PIPPIN CL.
B3181
ROAD (RING RD.)
WILTON WAY
MEMBURY CL.
DOTTON CL.
CHARD-STOCK CL.
A3015
HONITON RD.
6
EX1
CHARD LANE
SWEETBRIER LANE
CARLYON GDNS.
MADISON AV.
WHITEWAY DR.
NICHOLAS RD.
LYMEBORNE AV.
ROSELAND CRES.
Heavitree Pleasure Ground
Ten. Cts.
Pav.
Heavitree
RUSSET AV.
BRAMLEY AV.
RINGSWELL AV.
GARSIDE M.
St. Luke's High Sch.
BIRCHY BARTON HILL
WARWICK RD.
LWR. HILL BARTON RD.
ST. LAWRENCE CRES.
HONITON RD.
RINGSWELL PK.
NELSON WY.
SIDMOUTH RD.
HERON RD.
BITTERN RD.
CYGNET INDUSTRIAL UNITS
11
295
96
LONSDALE RD.
STANWEY
WHIPTON LA.

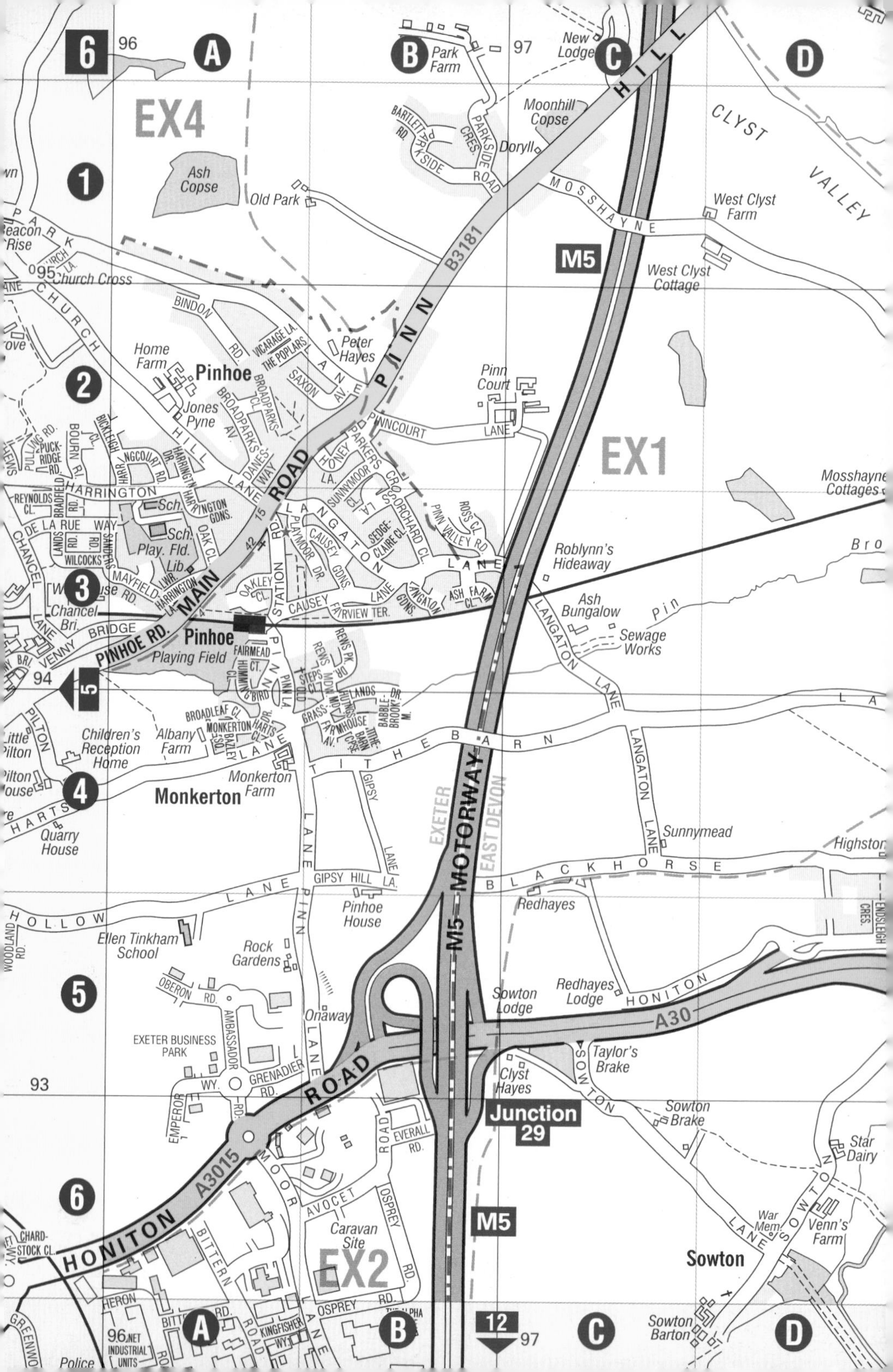

6
EX4
Pinhoe
Monkerton
EX1
EX2
Sowton
Pinhoe Playing Field
Park Farm
New Lodge
Moonhill Copse
Ash Copse
Old Park
Doryll
West Clyst Farm
West Clyst Cottage
CLYST VALLEY
Church Cross
Home Farm
Jones Pyne
Peter Hayes
Pinn Court
Mosshayne Cottages
Roblynn's Hideaway
Ash Bungalow
Sewage Works
Chancel Bri.
Children's Reception Home
Albany Farm
Monkerton Farm
Little Pilton
Pilton House
Quarry House
Sunnymead
Highston
Redhayes
Pinhoe House
Ellen Tinkham School
Rock Gardens
Onaway
Sowton Lodge
Redhayes Lodge
Taylor's Brake
Clyst Hayes
EXETER BUSINESS PARK
Sowton Brake
Star Dairy
Venn's Farm
War Mem.
Caravan Site
Sowton Barton
Junction 29
M5
M5 MOTORWAY
EXETER
EAST DEVON
PINN HILL
B3181
MAIN ROAD
PINHOE RD.
HONITON ROAD
A3015
A30
MOSSHAYNE
PARKSIDE ROAD
PARKSIDE CRES.
BARTLETT RD.
CHURCH LA.
CHURCH HILL
PARK
BINDON RD.
VICARAGE LA.
THE POPLARS
SAXON AV.
PINN LANE
BROADPARKS CL.
BROADPARKS AV.
DANES' WAY
HILL LANE
HONEY LA.
PARKERS CROSS LA.
PINNCOURT LANE
SUNNYMOOR CL.
ORCHARD CL.
SEDGE CL.
CLAIRE CL.
PINN VALLEY RD.
ROSS CL.
LANGATON LANE
LANGATON GDNS.
ASH FARM CL.
CAUSEY GDNS.
CAUSEY LANE
FAIRVIEW TER.
PLAYMOOR DR.
STATION RD.
OAKLEY CL.
OAK CL.
HARRINGTON GDNS.
HARRINGTON DR.
HARRINGTON LANE
LWR. HARRINGTON LA.
MAYFIELD RD.
WILCOCKS RD.
SANDERS RD.
LANDS RD.
DE LA RUE WAY
REYNOLDS CL.
BRADFIELD RD.
PUCKRIDGE RD.
PULLING RD.
BOURN RI.
BICKLEIGH CL.
CHANCEL LANE
VENNY BRIDGE
PILTON LANE
FAIRMEAD CT.
HUMMING BIRD CL.
PINN LA.
OLD STEPS CL.
REWS PK. DR.
REWS MDW.
GRASS MDW. AV.
FARMHOUSE AV.
LANDS DR.
BABBLEBROOK M.
TITHEBARN CPSE.
BROADLEAF CL.
MONKERTON DR.
HARTS CL.
BAZLEY SQ.
TITHEBARN LANE
HARTS LANE
GIPSY LANE
GIPSY HILL LA.
LANE
BLACKHORSE LANE
HOLLOW LANE
WOODLAND RD.
ENDSLEIGH CRES.
OBERON RD.
AMBASSADOR DR.
GRENADIER RD.
EMPEROR WY.
MOOR LANE
EVERALL RD.
AVOCET RD.
OSPREY RD.
BITTERN RD.
HERON RD.
KINGFISHER WY.
CHARDSTOCK CL.
NET INDUSTRIAL UNITS
SOWTON LANE
Pin
Bro
Police
93
94
95
96
97
5
12

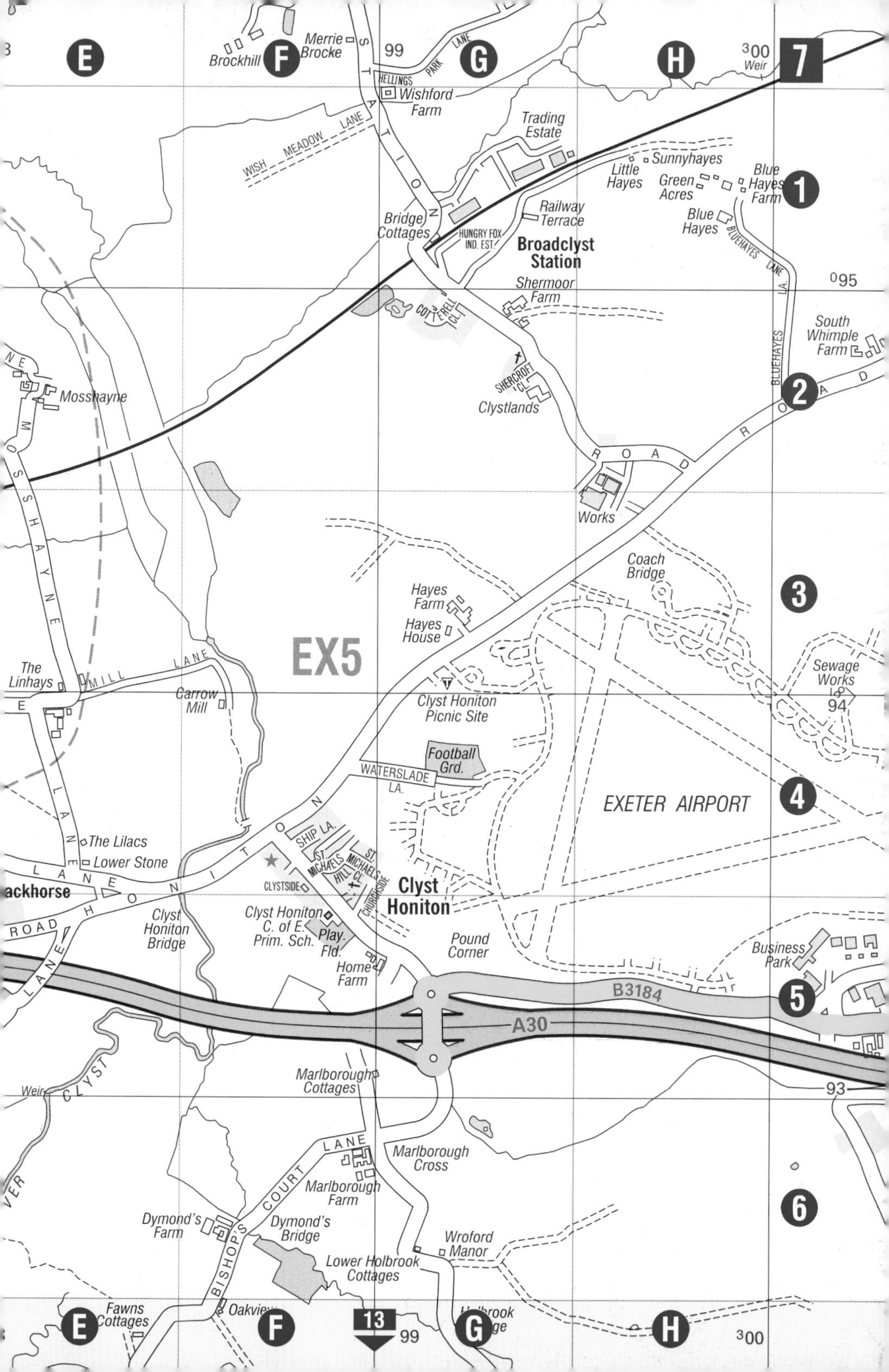
E
F
G
H
7
Brockhill
Merrie Brocke
99
300
Weir
STATION
HELLINGS PARK LANE
Wishford Farm
WISH MEADOW LANE
Trading Estate
Sunnyhayes
Little Hayes
Green Acres
Blue Hayes Farm
1
Railway Terrace
Bridge Cottages
HUNGRY FOX IND. EST.
Broadclyst Station
Blue Hayes
BLUEHAYES LANE
095
Shermoor Farm
COTTERELL CL.
South Whimple Farm
BLUEHAYES LA.
SHERCROFT CL.
Clystlands
2
ROAD
Mosshayne
MOSSHAYNE LANE
Works
Coach Bridge
3
Hayes Farm
Hayes House
EX5
Sewage Works
94
The Linhays
MILL LANE
Carrow Mill
Clyst Honiton Picnic Site
Football Grd.
WATERSLADE LA.
EXETER AIRPORT
4
HONITON
SHIP LA.
The Lilacs
Lower Stone
ST. MICHAELS
ST. MICHAELS HILL CL.
CHURCHSIDE
CLYSTSIDE
ackhorse
Clyst Honiton
Clyst Honiton C. of E. Prim. Sch.
Play. Fld.
Clyst Honiton Bridge
Pound Corner
Business Park
Home Farm
B3184
5
A30
CLYST
Weir
Marlborough Cottages
93
Marlborough Cross
Marlborough Farm
BISHOP'S COURT LANE
6
Dymond's Farm
Dymond's Bridge
Wroford Manor
Lower Holbrook Cottages
Fawns Cottages
Oakview
13
Holbrook
300

8
2
A
B
C
D
Alphin Brook
Cutteridge
Cutteridge Lane
Little Field Copse
Osbornes Farm
Broademore Plantation
Reservoir (covered)
Upper Old Wheatley Farm
Barley Lane
Bowhay
A30
Tedburn Road
Whorley Pin Plantation
Burnets Brakes
Eastwood
Eastdown Plantation
Nadder Brook
EX4
Westwood
Clattercleave House
Clattercleave Copse
Silverland Copse
Yonder Brake
West Wheatley Farm
Providence Court Farm
Wheatley
Larson Pl.
The Quarries
Barley Lane Sc.
Eagles Nest
Magpie Cres.
Sandpiper
Kingfisher Av.
Puffin Wy.
Heron Rd.
Swallow Dr.
Nightingale Wk.
Robin Grn.
Dove Wy.
Exonia Park
Cross Ha
Charlista
Black Hat Lane
Little Valley
Road Lane
Webby's Farm
EX6
Firs Park
Pocombe Bridge
Dunsford
Steep Acres
Mar-Cliff
B3212
Longdown Road
Mark's Cross
Mark's Farm
Hazeldene
Doctors Wlk.
Doctor's Wlk.
Scratch Face Lane
Tree Tops
Chillies Copse
Baker's Hill Lane
Haynes Farm
Haynes Road
Seven Acre Plantation
College Lane
New Buildings
Fordland Bottom Road
Fordland Brook
Fordland Bottom
Brook
Ide
Haynes Copse
Hendy Pl.
The Hams
The Green
Old Vicarage Cl.
Cobbe Ho.
Weir
Westown
Westown Road
West Town Farm
Earles Court
Station Road
St. Ida's Cl.
Pynes Cottages
Ide Brake
Rainbow Brake
Pollards Hill Brake
Whiddon Cottages
Halscombe
Lane
Dunchideock
Idestone Lane
Whiddon Farm
Whiddon
Whiddon Cottages
Ma
1
2
3
4
5
6
92
91
90
88
89

E
F
G
H
9
3
Redhills
EXETER
Dinham
BONHAY RD.
A377
WESTERN WY.
1
2
3
4
5
6
Friars Green
Larkbear
Haven Banks
INDUSTRIAL ESTATE
St.Thomas
Leisure Cen.
St.Thomas Pleasure Grd.
COWICK STREET
COWICK ROAD
COWICK LANE
County Grd. Stadium
FRANKLYN HOSP.
B3212
DUNSFORD
St. Thomas
Cowick Barton Playing Field
Pleasure Gardens
GX Superbowl
26
ALPHINGTON ROAD
ALPHINGTON ST.
10
91
Ide House
Saw Mill
Ide Bridge
Underwood
Ball's Farm
Cloon
The Briars
Nursery
Oak Marsh Farm
Ide First School
EX2
A30
A377
ALPHINGTON SPUR
CHURCH RD.
B3123
ALPHIN BROOK RD.
Alphington
Alphington Bri.
Playing Field
St.Thomas High Sch.
Cricket Ground
TEIGNBRIDGE
EXETER
CHUDLEIGH RD.
Silverlands
Elldor
Montego
Barnfield House
14
92

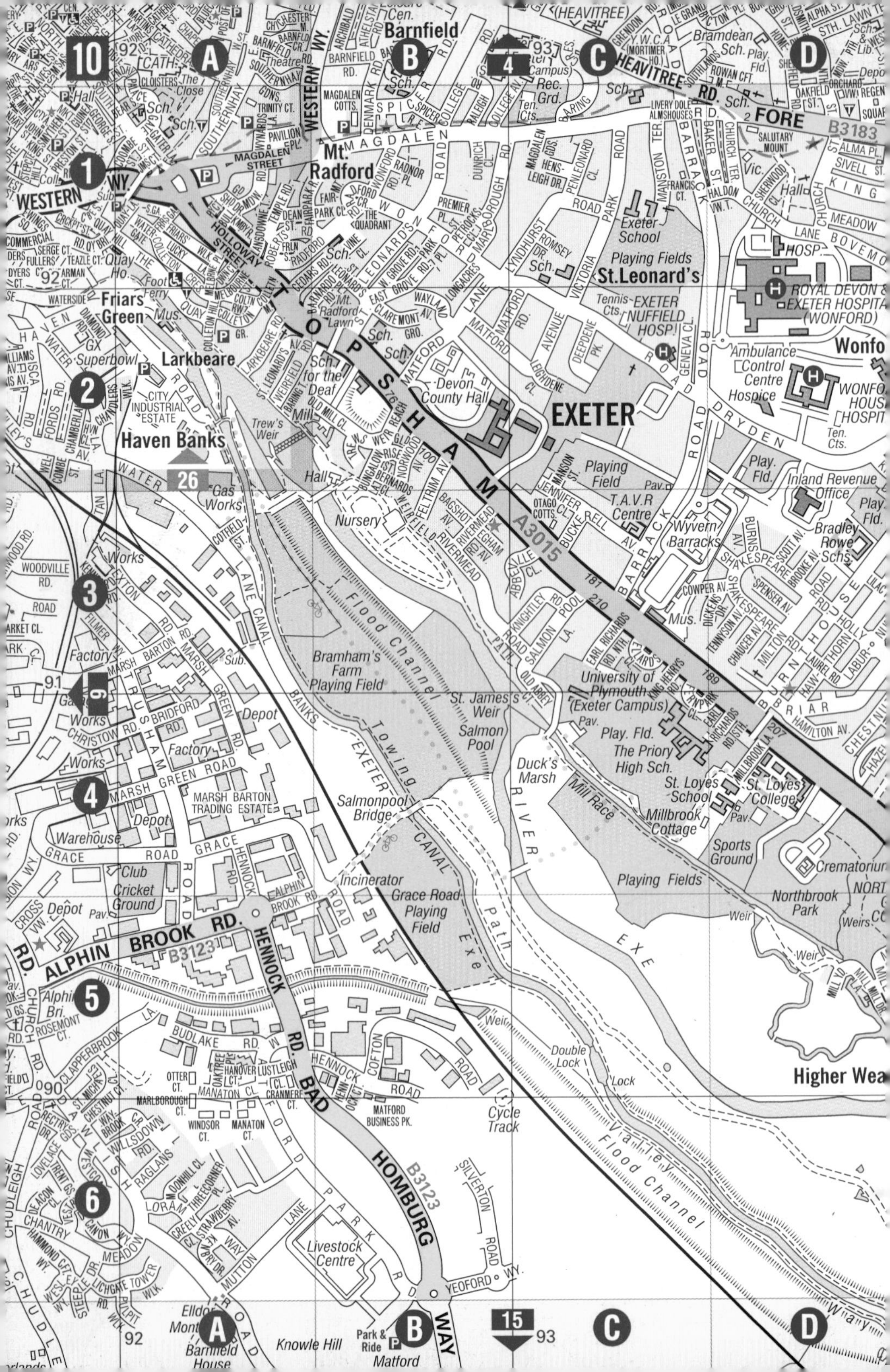

10
A
B
C
D
1
2
3
4
5
6
92
93
91
90
Barnfield
Mt. Radford
St. Leonard's
EXETER
Friars Green
Larkbeare
Haven Banks
Wonford
Higher Wear
HEAVITREE RD.
FORE
B3183
MAGDALEN STREET
MAGDALEN
WESTERN WY.
WESTERN
HOLLOWAY STREET
TOPSHAM
A3015
BARRACK ROAD
DRYDEN
WONFORD
ALPHIN BROOK RD.
B3123
HENNOCK RD.
BAD HOMBURG WAY
GRACE ROAD
MARSH GREEN ROAD
MARSH BARTON TRADING ESTATE
CITY INDUSTRIAL ESTATE
Exeter School
Playing Fields
EXETER NUFFIELD HOSP.
ROYAL DEVON & EXETER HOSPITAL (WONFORD)
Ambulance Control Centre
Hospice
Devon County Hall
Sch. for the Deaf
Wyvern Barracks
T.A.V.R Centre
Inland Revenue Office
Bradley Rowe Schs.
University of Plymouth (Exeter Campus)
The Priory High Sch.
St. Loyes School
St. Loyes College
Millbrook Cottage
Sports Ground
Crematorium
Northbrook Park
Duck's Marsh
Mill Race
RIVER EXE
Flood Channel
Bramham's Farm Playing Field
St. James's Weir
Salmon Pool
Salmonpool Bridge
Incinerator
Grace Road Playing Field
Exeter Canal
Towing Path
Double Lock
Cycle Track
Valley Flood Channel
Gas Works
Trew's Weir
Nursery
Livestock Centre
MATFORD BUSINESS PK.
Club Cricket Ground
Warehouse
Depot
Factory
Works
Superbowl
Quay Ho.
Foot Ferry
Mus.
26
9
4
15
Knowle Hill
Park & Ride
Matford
Barnfield House

Heavitree
EX1
EX2
HONITON ROAD
B3183
WONFORD HILL
EAST WONFORD
STREET
SIDMOUTH RD.
(RING-ROAD)
LANE
A3015
A379
RYDON LANE
ROAD
BRIDGE ROAD
OLD RYDON
St. Luke's High Sch.
Police Training Centre
Civil Defence H.Q.
Southam
St. Peter's C. of E. High Sch. & Sports Centre
Sports Ground
Hotel
Peninsula House
Walter Daw First Sch.
St.Loye's
Chestnut Avenue Nursery Sch.
Wonford Sports Cen.
Mushroom Farm Nurseries
RYDON PARK CARAVAN PARK
Park & Ride
Digby & Sowton
Superstore
Pynes Hill
LUDWELL VALLEY PARK
Playing Fields
Southbrook School
St Bridget Nurseries
Beech Cottage
Builder's Yard
Vitacop
Wynards Cottages
Weir View
Lavender Lodge
Royal Naval Depot
The West of England School for Children With Little or No Sight
Vicarage
EXETER GOLF COURSE AND COUNTRY CLUB
Exeter & District Community Health Service N.H.S. Trust H.Q.
King George V Playing Field
Countess Wear
Mount Wear Youth Hostel
Club Ho.
ROYAL NAVAL DEPOT
Golf Course
Linkways
Countess Weir Combined School
Playing Field
Comm. Cen.
Lower Wear
Countess Wear Bri.
Seabrook House
Sandy Park
Nurseries
M5
5
16
11
12
295
96
92
91
090
95
E F G H
1 2 3 4 5 6

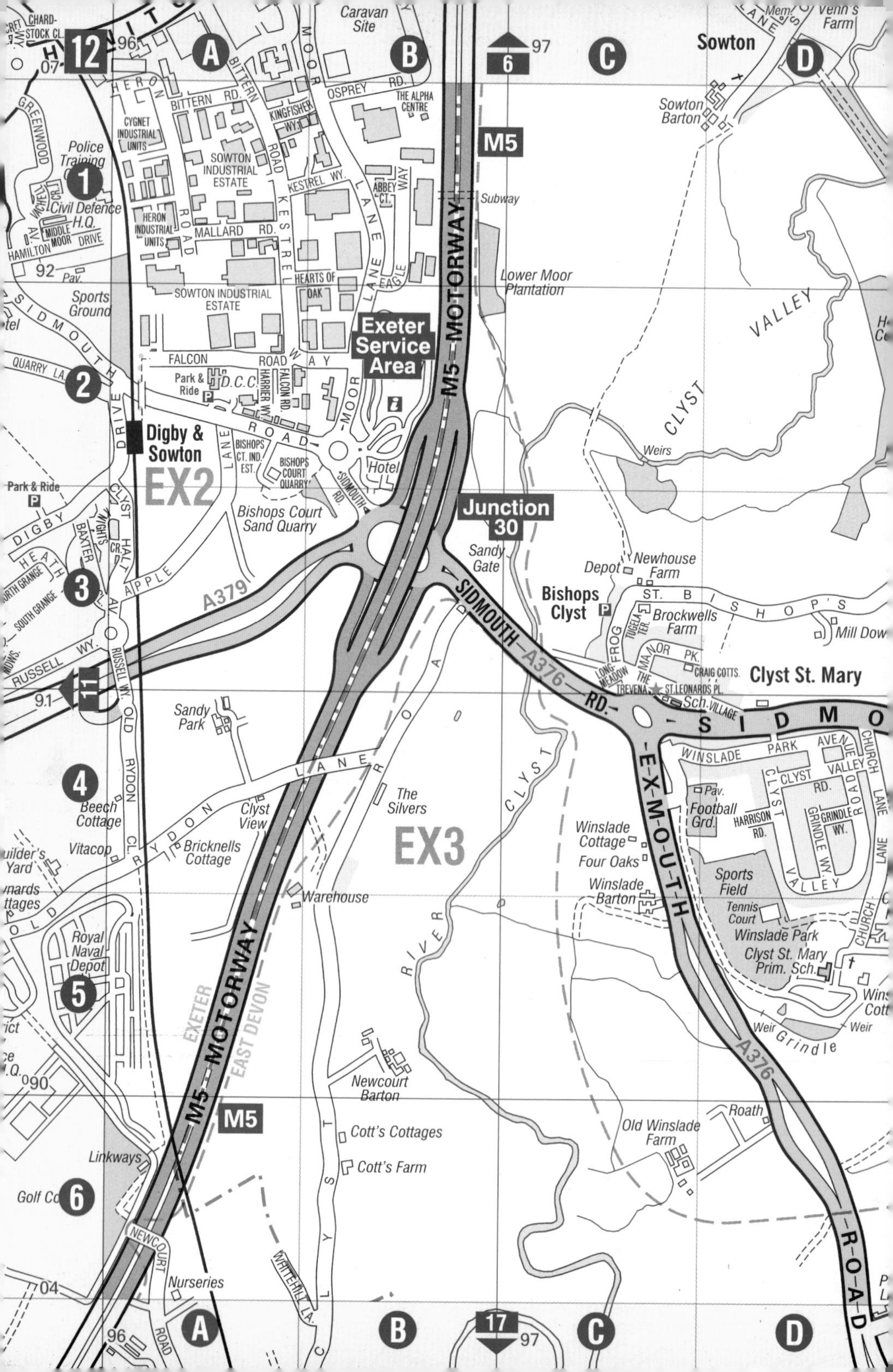

12
A
B
C
D
6
97
17
Caravan Site
Sowton
Venn's Farm
Sowton Barton
Police Training
Civil Defence H.Q.
Sports Ground
CYGNET INDUSTRIAL UNITS
SOWTON INDUSTRIAL ESTATE
HERON INDUSTRIAL UNITS
THE ALPHA CENTRE
HEARTS OF OAK
BITTERN RD.
OSPREY RD.
KINGFISHER WY.
KESTREL WY.
MALLARD RD.
FALCON ROAD
FALCON RD.
HARRIER WY.
ABBEY CT.
HAMILTON DRIVE
MIDDLE MOOR
SIDMOUTH
QUARRY LA.
Park & Ride
D.C.C.
Digby & Sowton
EX2
Exeter Service Area
Hotel
BISHOPS CT. IND. EST.
BISHOPS COURT QUARRY
Bishops Court Sand Quarry
M5
MOTORWAY
M5 MOTORWAY
Subway
Lower Moor Plantation
CLYST VALLEY
Weirs
Junction 30
Sandy Gate
Depot
Newhouse Farm
Bishops Clyst
ST. BISHOP'S
Brockwells Farm
Mill Down
MANOR PK.
CRAIG COTTS.
ST. LEONARDS PL.
Clyst St. Mary
A379
A376
SIDMOUTH RD.
DIGBY
CLYST HALT
APPLE
RUSSELL WY.
OLD RYDON CL.
RYDON LANE
Sandy Park
Beech Cottage
Vitacop
Clyst View
Bricknells Cottage
The Silvers
EX3
Warehouse
RIVER CLYST
WINSLADE PARK AVENUE
CLYST VALLEY RD.
Football Grd.
Sports Field
Tennis Court
Winslade Park
Clyst St. Mary Prim. Sch.
Winslade Cottage
Four Oaks
Winslade Barton
EXMOUTH ROAD
Royal Naval Depot
EXETER
EAST DEVON
Newcourt Barton
Cott's Cottages
Cott's Farm
Roath
Old Winslade Farm
Linkways
Golf Co
NEWCOURT
Nurseries
WHITEHILL LA.
Grindle
Weir

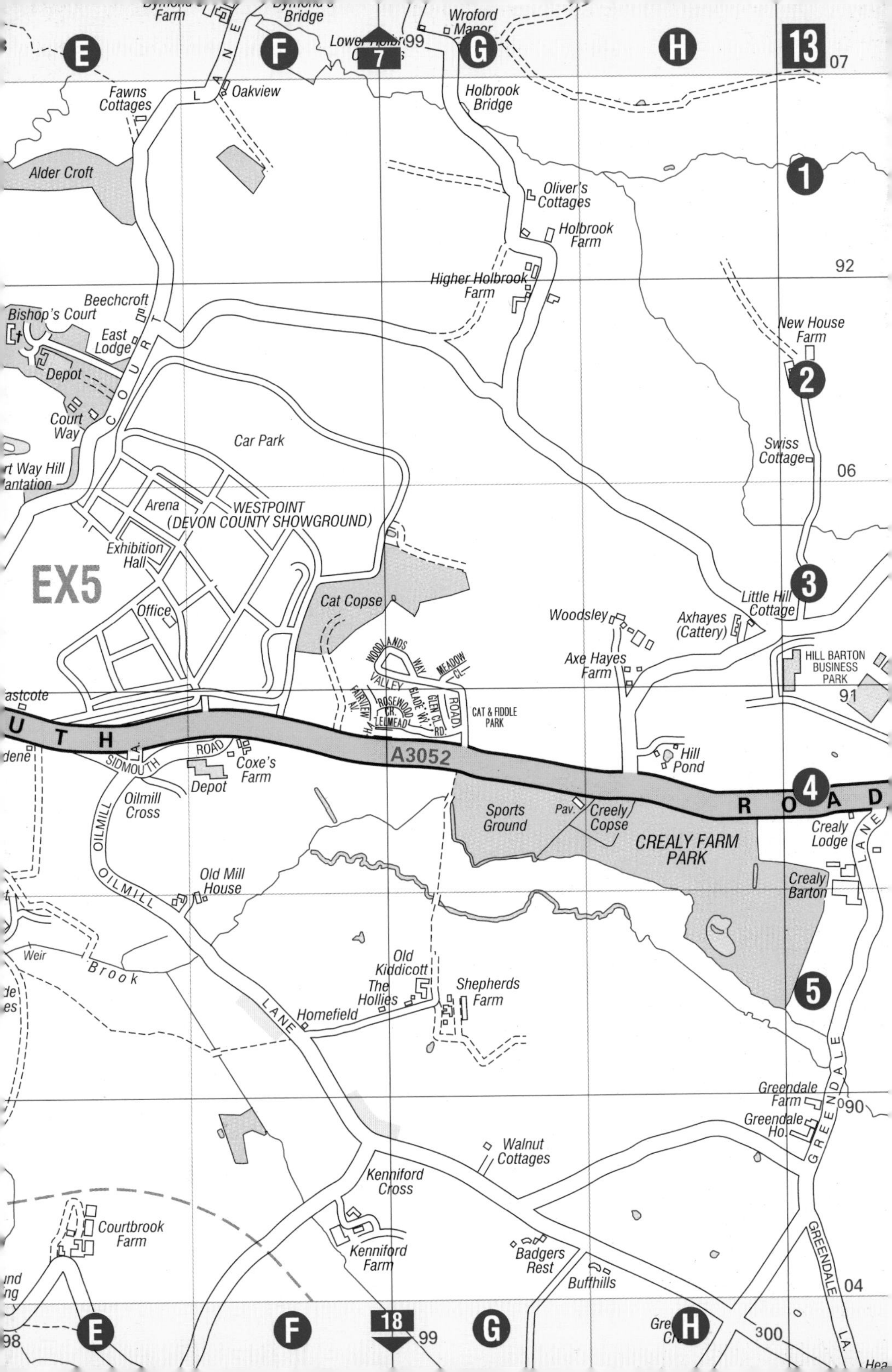

Fawns Cottages
Oakview
Wroford Manor
Holbrook Bridge
Alder Croft
Oliver's Cottages
Holbrook Farm
Higher Holbrook Farm
Beechcroft
Bishop's Court
East Lodge
Depot
Court Way
New House Farm
Swiss Cottage
Car Park
Arena
WESTPOINT (DEVON COUNTY SHOWGROUND)
Exhibition Hall
EX5
Cat Copse
Office
Little Hill Cottage
Woodsley
Axhayes (Cattery)
Axe Hayes Farm
HILL BARTON BUSINESS PARK
CAT & FIDDLE PARK
A3052
Hill Pond
SIDMOUTH ROAD
Coxe's Farm
Depot
Oilmill Cross
Sports Ground
Pav.
Creely Copse
CREALY FARM PARK
Crealy Lodge
Crealy Barton
OILMILL LANE
Old Mill House
Weir
Brook
Old Kiddicott
The Hollies
Shepherds Farm
Homefield
Greendale Farm
Greendale Ho.
GREENDALE LANE
Walnut Cottages
Kenniford Cross
Courtbrook Farm
Kenniford Farm
Badgers Rest
Bufthills
300

7
18

MARKHAM LANE
POLEHOUSE LA.
A30
SHILLINGFORD ROAD
BARNSTONE CT.
Silverlands
ROYAL VEITCH CL.
WESLEY WY.
STEELE DR.
CHUDLEIGH LANE
MARKHAM LANE
WAYBROOK COTTAGES
The Bungalow
LOWER SHILLINGFORD
OAK CL.
WAYBROOK
Shillingford Lodge
Pengellys
BARRACK LA.
Shillingford Abbot
Haldon View
Hamlyn's Cottages
Keeper's Cottage
Bowhay Farm
The Barton
Barton Cottage
BARTON
Peamore Wood
Bowhay Cottage
EX2
Crosslands
War Mem.
Peamore Lodge
Bathing Pit Bottom
Shillingford St. George
Shillingford Plantation
Peamore House Hotel
Cattle Grid
MANSTREE RD.
MANSTREE TER.
THE WILLOWS
ASH CT.
ST. GEORGE'S TER.
ILEX CL.
Glebe Mead
SAMPSON'S
The Rock
New Barn Farm
Rec. Grd.
South View Farm
Glebe Farm
Pond Wood
Orchard Cottage
HILL
Shillingford Wood
Place Farm
Dadmouth
SHILLINGFORD LANE
A379
Clapham
Linslade
Lower Brenton
Morway
OLD
Reservoir (Covered)
BRENTON ROAD
Higher Brenton
TWO STONE LA.
River Kenn
BEERS TER.
Quarry Copse
A38
KENNFORD
RAYNERS
SANDFORDS
A B C D
1 2 3 4 5 6
9

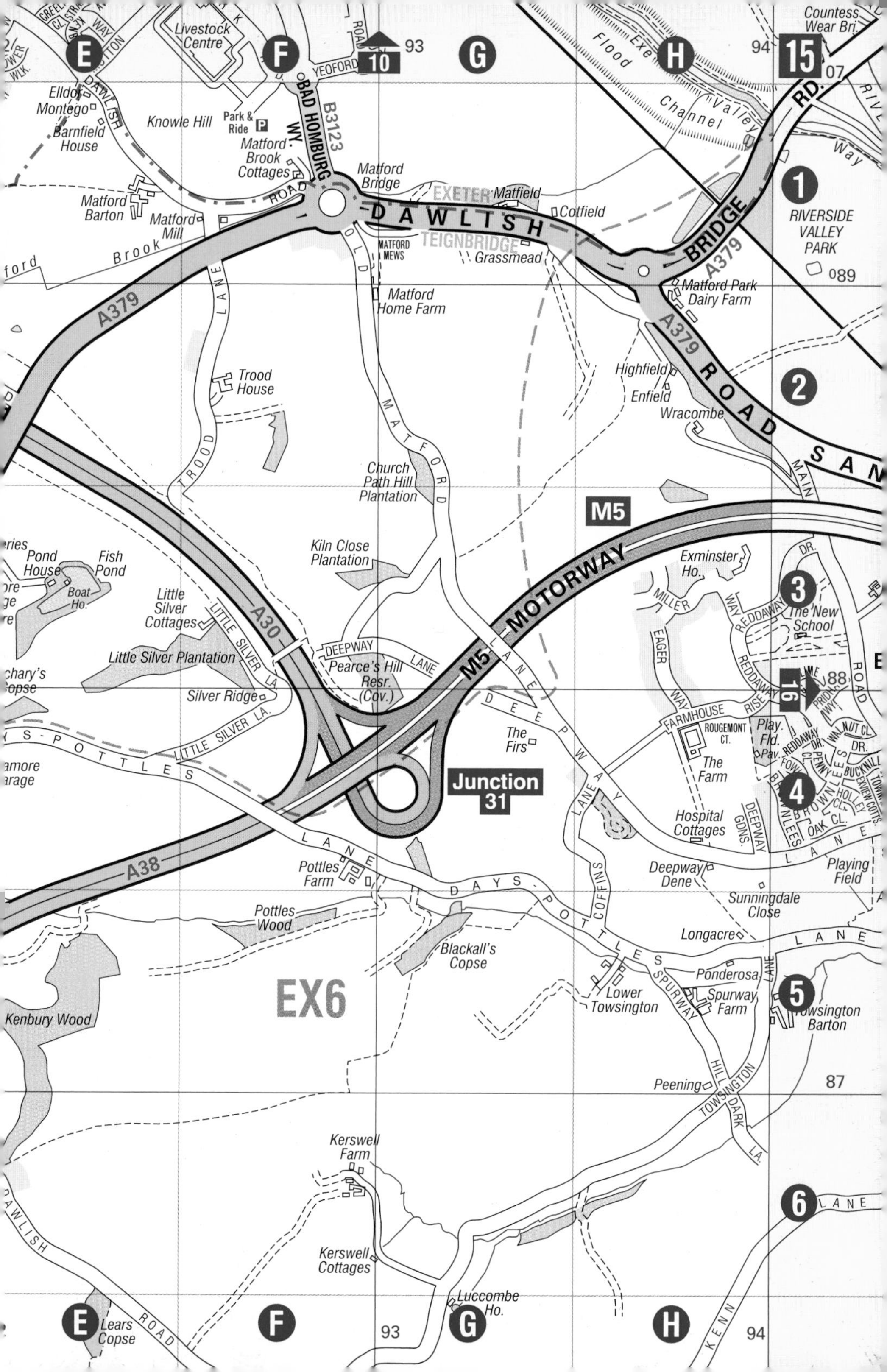

15
10
16
E
F
G
H
1
2
3
4
5
6
93
94
07
089
88
87
Livestock Centre
Elldon
Montego
Barnfield House
Knowle Hill
Park & Ride
Matford Brook Cottages
BAD HOMBURG WY.
B3123
YEOFORD
Matford Bridge
Matford Barton
Matford Mill
Brook
DAWLISH ROAD
EXETER
TEIGNBRIDGE
Matfield
Cotfield
Grassmead
MATFORD MEWS
Matford Home Farm
Countess Wear Bri.
Flood Channel
Exe Valley Way
BRIDGE RD.
A379
RIVERSIDE VALLEY PARK
Matford Park Dairy Farm
A379 ROAD
Highfield
Enfield
Wracombe
SAM
MAIN
Trood House
TROOD LANE
MATFORD
Church Path Hill Plantation
M5
Kiln Close Plantation
M5 MOTORWAY
Exminster Ho.
MILLER
WAY
REDDAWAY
The New School
EAGER WAY
REDDAWAY RISE
ROAD
Pond House
Fish Pond
Boat Ho.
Little Silver Cottages
LITTLE SILVER LA.
A30
Little Silver Plantation
DEEPWAY LANE
Pearce's Hill Resr. (Cov.)
Silver Ridge
LANE
DEEPWAY
FARMHOUSE
ROUGEMONT CT.
The Farm
Play. Fld.
Pav.
WALNUT CL.
BUCKNILL
PENNY
HOLLEY
OAK CL.
BROWNLEES
The Firs
Junction 31
Hospital Cottages
GDNS.
LANE
Playing Field
A38
Pottles Farm
DAYS-POTTLES LANE
COFFINS LANE
Deepway Dene
Sunningdale Close
Pottles Wood
Blackall's Copse
Longacre
Ponderosa
Lower Towsington
SPURWAY
Spurway Farm
Towsington Barton
EX6
Kenbury Wood
HILL
Peening
TOWSINGTON
DARK LA.
Kerswell Farm
Kerswell Cottages
DAWLISH ROAD
Luccombe Ho.
Lears Copse
KENN

Countess Wear Bri.
Lower Wear
ROYAL NAVAL DEPOT
EX2
Seabrook House
Newport Lodge
Football Grd.
NEWPORT PARK
RIVERSIDE VALLEY PARK
Sewage Works
Tumbling Hills
Playing Field
Comm. Cen.
Matford Park Dairy Farm
Old Sludge Beds Nature Reserve
M5 MOTORWAY
The Retreat
Towing Path
Mud
Wracombe
SANNERVILLE WAY
A379
M5
Exminster Ho.
Milbury Farm
The New School
EXMINSTER
TEIGNBRIDGE
EXETER
EX6
The Farm
Hospital Cottages
Playing Field
Spurfield
Almshouses
Sunningdale Close
Longacre
Ponderosa
Pitts House
Towsington Barton
Vine Cott.
EXMINSTER MARSHES
BIRD SANCTUARY
Higher Marshrow
MAIN ROAD
STATION ROAD
MARSHROW LANE
KENN LANE
EXMINSTER LANE
DEEPWAY
DAWLISH RD.
BRIDGE RD.
TOPSHAM RD.
EXETER ROAD
MILBURY LANE
94
295
088
88
87
15
11

E
F
G
H
12
97
98
17
EXMOUTH
A376
Pound Living
Whitehill Lane
Clyst
Highfield
Morwenna
Broom Park Nurseries
Five Acres
Highfield Farm
Sunhill
Water Tower
Cemetery
Creadly
Grove Hill
Lane
Court Farm
Marsh Lane
Knowle House
Fire Brigade Headquarters
Road
EAST DEVON
EXETER
EX3
Topsham
Lib.
Sch.
Playing Field
Ferry Road
High Street
Fore Street
Weir
Bridge Mill
Marsh Barton
Depot
Boat Yard
Clyst Bridge
Odams Wharf
18
88
Topsham Lock
Landing Stages
Ferry
Wharves
TOPSHAM
Topsham Quay
Four Winds
Western Fields
Allways
Ebford Manor
Mount Ebford
Causeway
Mus.
Strand
Mount Howe
BOWLING GREEN MARSH NATURE RESERVE
Causeways
Landing Stage
Goat Walk
Riversmeet
Riversmeet House
Boat House
RIVER CLYST
Hampstead La.
Upway
Woodbury House
Red Hills
87
Canal
Towing Path
RIVER EXE
Green La.
Shorthill
Exton
Exton La.
River
Front
Sandpiper Dr.
96
97
98

18
Courtbrook Farm
Kenniford Farm
13
99
Badgers Rest
Buffhills
Greendale Cross
A376
Ford
Weir
PYTTE GS.
Pytte House
Clyst St. George
Heathfield Farm
Roymar Farm
WOODBURY
MARSH LANE
Knowle House
Fire Brigade Headquarters
RECTORY GDNS.
Rec.
Lady Seawards C. of E. Prim. Sch.
The Cottage
ROAD
Marlanne Pool
Bushayes Farm
WOODBURY
Postlake Farm
Marsh Barton
Depot
Yard
EX3
MOOR LANE
MOOR
Branscombe Farm
88
17
Ebford
Riding School
EBFORD
EBFORD LANE
OLD
Lane Side
Meadow Cott.
B3179
Ebford Barton
Ebford Manor
Allways
Mount Ebford
Fish Ponds
Higher Bagmores Farm
South Hill Farm
EXMOUTH
EXMOUTH ROAD
Coppins
Greensleeves
HAMPSTEAD LANE
Pinehurst
Hillside
Wood Cottages
Red Hills
Lower Bagmores Farm
Upway
87
House
Rydon Farm
GREEN LANE
Shorthill
EXTON LA.
EXTON
Rydon Mill Farm
MILL LANE
RIVER
Exton
Whinfield Nursery
Exton Mill
RYDON
98
SANDPIPER DR.
FRONT
BARTON CT.
Exton Fm.
MILL LANE
Exton
STA. R.
99
A
B
C
D
1
2
3
4
5
6

E
F
G
H
01
02
Grindle Brook
Depot
LANE
Industrial Estate
GREENDALE LA.
Sewage Works
Bidgood's Farm
Heathfield Cross
Heathfield House
LOWER ROAD
Castleton
Heathfield Plot
HIGHER
PARKHAYES
HONEY
Honey Cottage
Woodbury Salterton
Football Ground
Higher Downhams
VILLAGE ROAD
Sch.
089
STONY LANE
NEW WY.
Bridge Farm
CROSS ROAD
WHITE
Higher Pilehayes Farm
Cooks Farm
Cannonwalls Farm
Trevanin Farm
Pilehayes Farm
Pigeons Farm
Browns Farm
06
Willowmead
LANE
The Firs
EX5
Stocklet Haven
Buckfield
88
Bond Farm House
Deepway Farm
BONDS
WATERY LANE
Parsonage House
Cottles
COTTLES LANE
Cottles Farm
Res.
Vic.
WAY
Cemy.
SUMMERFIELD
POUND LA.
BAKER GRO.
LONG PARK
LONGMEADOW
PARSONAGE
GOVERTS
CASTLE LANE
OAKHAYES
Webber's Farm
Shepherds Park Farm
Oakhayes
Prim. Sch.
WEBBER'S FARM CARAVAN PARK
BONFIRE
CULVERY CL.
LA.
BROADMEAD
MIREY LA.
ORCHARD CL.
Burstone House
Rec. Grd.
Woodbury Wood
FLOWER ST.
STILE LA.
TOWN LANE
Springhayes
BRENT CLOSE
BRETTEVILLE CL.
Woodbury
87
THE ARCH
CHURCH
GREENWAY
FULFORD
FURZE RD.
GLOBE HILL
BROADWAY
ROAD
CRITCHARDS
PARK CL.
BEECHES CL.
PARK WY.
Woodbury Mills
Hill's Venmoor
Ford Farm
B3179
Higher Venmoor Farm
Downs Corner
Bridge Pitt Farm
Venmore Farm
300
1
2
3
4
5
6

A
B
C
D
1
2
3
4
5
6
99
300
85
84
83
82
Nutwell Court
Nutwell Park
Bower Shrubbery
Daniel's Corner
Belvedere
Hayes Raleigh
Lympstone Village
Play. Fld.
Pier
Lympstone
The Rectory
Candys
Manor Ho.
Prim. Sch.
Lympstone Ho.
Gulliford
Burial Ground
Nurseries
Lodge
Tedstone House
Middle Coombe Cottage
Rising Sun Cottage
Thorn Farm
St. Peters School
Ten. Ct.
Playing Field
Lower Coombe Farm
Ford
Brook
Monday Copse
Coombe Farm
Wotton Pound
Watton Bridge
Watton Farm
Wotton House
Watton
Brook
Ford
The Mill
Mount Pleasant
Southtown Ho.
Sowden Farm
Atlantis
Mussel Purification Station
Long Park
Nurseries
North Lodge
East Lodge
Courtlands
West Lodge
Linhayes Farm
Potter's Farm
Pitt Farm
EX8
Backenhayes
Marley Riding Stable
Summerfield House
Courtlands Cross
Three Acres
The Point in View
Manse
A-la-Ronde (National Trust)
Hulham
Sand & Mud
Higher Halsdown Farm
Lower Halsdown Farm
Warren View Sports Grd.
Social Club
Pav.
Rayleigh Park
Play. Fld.
Exmouth Community College (Upper Site)
King George V
Cockle Sand
22
EXMOUTH ROAD
EXETER ROAD
A376
JUBILEE GRO.
NUTWELL ROAD
HAREFIELD ROAD
HAREFIELD LANE
TEDSTONE LANE
MEETING HILL
BURGMANNS HILL
EDINBURGH CRES.
CHURCHILL CT.
GIBRALTAR RD.
TRAFALGAR
GLEBELANDS
GLEBE CL.
HUNTON CL.
STRAWBERRY HILL
ORCHARD CL.
GRANGE CL.
BIRCH RD.
CANDY'S AV.
SCHOOL HILL
GREENHILL
CHURCH ROAD
LONGMEADOW ROAD
STONE LA.
HAREFIELD DR.
MEADOW CL.
MATFIELD
WOTTON LANE
THE STRAND
CHAPEL RD.
UNDERHILL
UNDERHILL CRES.
BRIDGES CR.
SOWDEN LANE
HIGHCLIFFE CL.
CLAY LANE
LONGBROOK
COURTLANDS LANE
DAWLISH PK. TER.
SUMMER LANE
LITTLEMEAD
HILL DRIVE
OAK TREE CL.
THORPE AV.
APPLE CL.
WOODLANDS CT.
WOODLANDS DR.
PLEASANT
SWISS CL.
APRIL CL.
MOUNT
WILLOW AV.
ESSINGTON CL.
ESSINGTON CT.
AVENUE
LAMPLOUGH RD.
RIVERMEAD AV.
SYLVAN CL.
ELMFIELD
ELMFIELD CRES.
ASH GRO.
CRESCENT
MOUNT-PLEASANT CT.
ROUNDHOUSE LA.
LANE
SEAFIELD AV.
THORNFIELD CL.
FEATHERBED LANE
FEATHERSTONE RD.
IONA AV.
SEYMOUR RD.
SEYMOUR CT.
TURNBULL CT.
SCOTT
BAPTON CLOSE
HALDON CT.
MARISTOW AV.
CAULESTON CL.
MORVEN DR.
EAST DR.
ORCHARD CL.
BAPTON ROAD
KEVERELL RD.
PHILLIPPS
HALSDON LANE
CROSSING-FIELDS DR.
HIGHBURY PK.
CARBERRY AV.
HALSDON AVENUE
TRINFIELD AV.
SPRINGFIELD
HAZELDENE GS.
AVENUE
BURNSIDE
NUTBROOK
BELLE VUE RD.
KINGSLAND CT.
BEECHWAY
GRANGE AV.
GIPSY
DENING CT.
WITHY

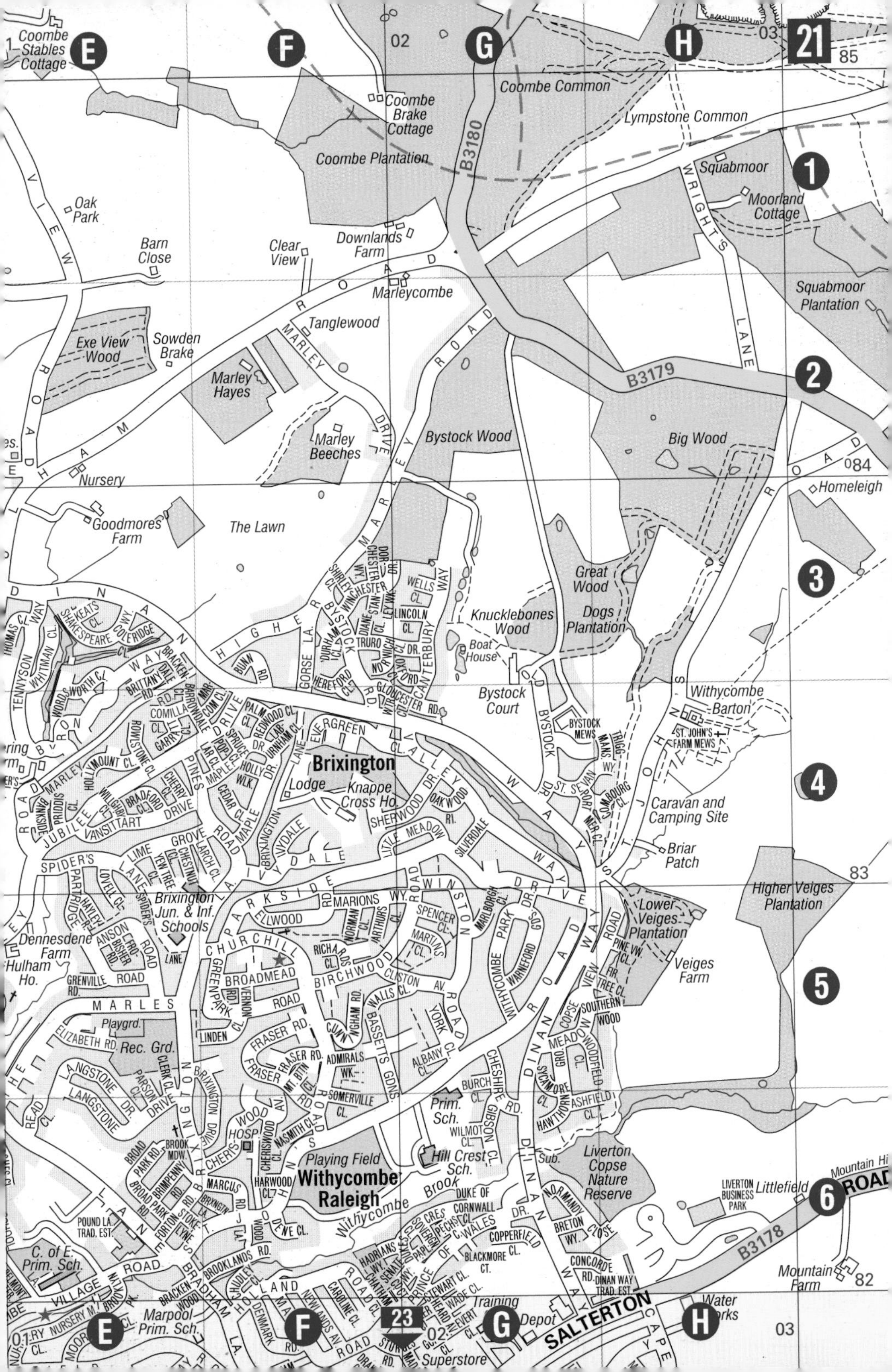

Coombe Stables Cottage
Coombe Brake Cottage
Coombe Plantation
Coombe Common
Lympstone Common
Squabmoor
Moorland Cottage
Squabmoor Plantation
Oak Park
Barn Close
Clear View
Downlands Farm
Marleycombe
Tanglewood
Exe View Wood
Sowden Brake
Marley Hayes
Marley Beeches
Bystock Wood
Big Wood
Homeleigh
Nursery
Goodmores Farm
The Lawn
Great Wood
Dogs Plantation
Knucklebones Wood
Boat House
Bystock Court
Withycombe Barton
St. John's Farm Mews
Brixington
Lodge
Knappe Cross Ho.
Caravan and Camping Site
Briar Patch
Higher Veiges Plantation
Lower Veiges Plantation
Veiges Farm
Brixington Jun. & Inf. Schools
Dennesdene Farm
Hulham Ho.
Playgrd.
Rec. Grd.
Prim. Sch.
Hill Crest Sch.
Playing Field
Withycombe Raleigh
Withycombe Brook
Liverton Copse Nature Reserve
Liverton Business Park
Littlefield
Mountain Farm
Pound La. Trad. Est.
C. of E. Prim. Sch.
Marpool Prim. Sch.
Training Depot
Water Works
Superstore
Dinan Way Trad. Est.
Salterton
B3180
B3179
B3178

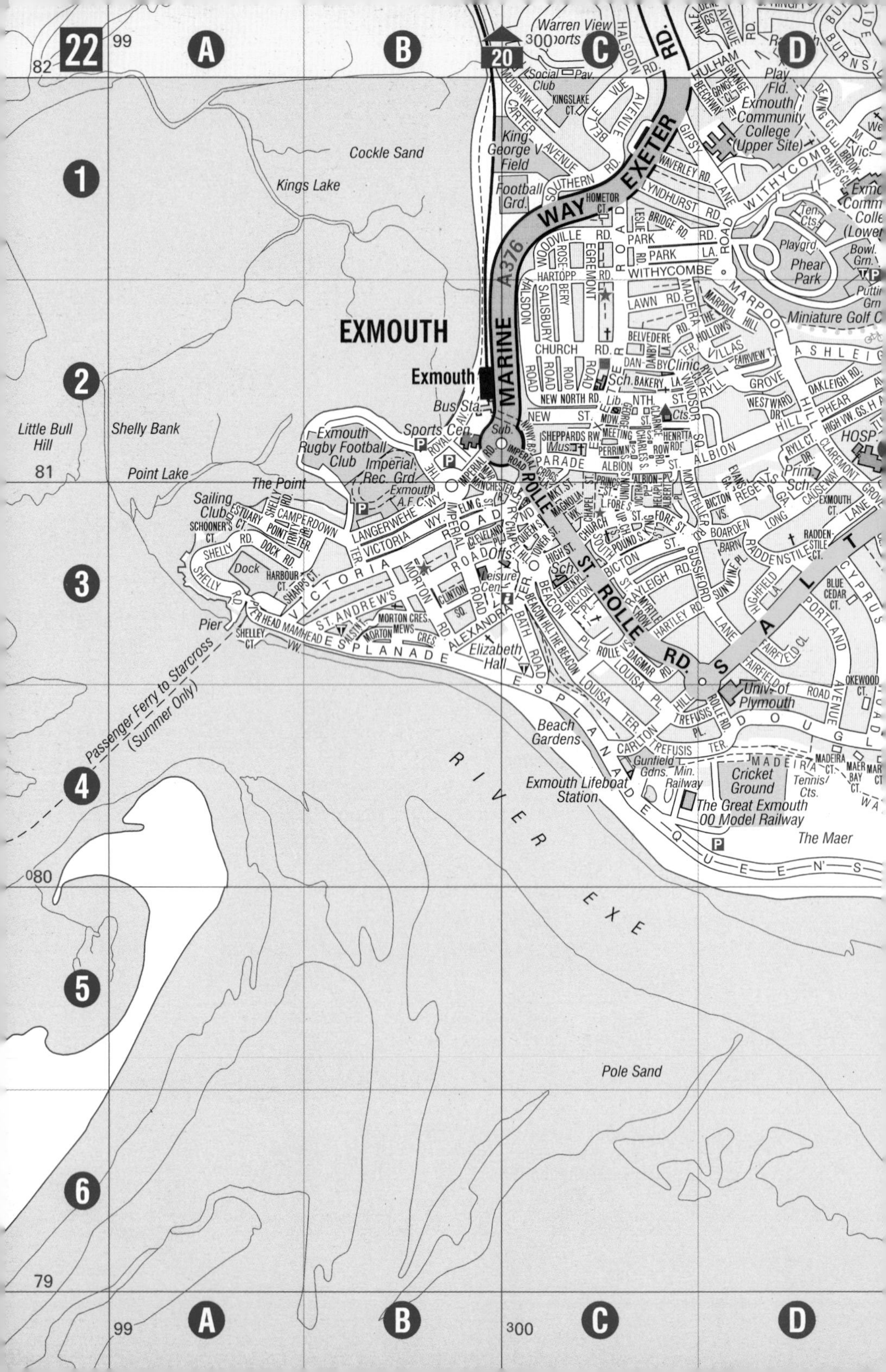
A
B
C
D
1
2
3
4
5
6
99
300
82
81
080
79
20
EXMOUTH
Exmouth
Cockle Sand
Kings Lake
Little Bull Hill
Shelly Bank
Point Lake
The Point
Sailing Club
Exmouth Rugby Football Club
Imperial Rec. Grd.
Exmouth A.F.C.
Sports Cen.
Bus Sta.
King George V Field
Football Grd.
Warren View Sports
Social Club
Pav.
Play Fld.
Exmouth Community College (Upper Site)
Phear Park
Playgrd.
Miniature Golf C
Clinic
Lib.
Mus.
Cts.
Leisure Cen.
Offs.
Dock
Pier
Elizabeth Hall
Beach Gardens
Univ. of Plymouth
Cricket Ground
Tennis Cts.
Gunfield Gdns.
Min. Railway
Exmouth Lifeboat Station
The Great Exmouth 00 Model Railway
The Maer
Passenger Ferry to Starcross (Summer Only)
RIVER EXE
Pole Sand
HOSP.
Prim. Sch.
EXETER RD.
MARINE WAY
A376
WITHYCOMBE ROAD
ST. ROLLE RD.
ROLLE ST.
SALTERTON RD.
ESPLANADE
VICTORIA ROAD
ALEXANDRA TER.
MADEIRA
DOUGLAS
QUEEN'S

23
21
E
F
G
H
1
2
3
4
5
6
02
03
82
81
080
79
EX8
B3178
Littleham
C. of E. Prim. Sch.
Marpool Prim. Sch.
Training Cen.
Depot
Superstore
Water Works
Mountain Farm
Cemetery
Littleham Brook
Leisure Cen.
Works
Playing Field
Littleham C. of E. Prim. Sch.
Sch.
Hall
Sports Club
Tennis Cts.
Green Farm
Prattshayes
Prattshayes Farm
Ford
Crowden Plantation
Sewage Works
Maer Farm
Swim. Pool
Hotel
Maer Bridge
Clayhill Cottages
Res.
Golf Range
Maer Rocks
Rodney Steps
Rodney Point
Devil's Ledge
Orcombe Rocks
Orcombe Point
Coastguard Lookout
High Land of Orcombe
Sandy Bay
ROAD
LITTLEHAM
CAPEL LANE
ROSEWAY
NELSON DRIVE
MAGNOLIA AV.
SUMMER BERRY CL.
THE GREEN
JARVIS CL.
BUCKINGHAM CL.
BARNFIELD AV.
AVENUE
ELVIS RD.
RICHMOND RD.
CHICHESTER CL.
COLLETON CLOSE
MARPOOL CRES.
MOORFIELD CL.
BRADHAM LANE
MASEY RD.
NEWLANDS AV.
DRAKE'S AV.
BROADWAY
ORCOMBE CT.
CRANFORD AV.
MERRION AV.
MAYFIELD DR.
STEVENSTONE RD.
SARLSDOWN RD.
ELWYN RD.
MEETWAYS LANE
RANDELL'S GREEN
MAER LANE
GORSE LANE
MAER ROAD
FOXHOLES HILL
QUEEN'S DRIVE
THOMAS CL.
CASTLE LANE
WEST DOWN LA.
MEAD COTTS.
CAPEL COTTS.
ST. MARGARET'S VW.
RODNEY CL.
ELM LA.
GLEBE CL.
LITTLEDOWN
PANKHURST CL.
HUDSON WAY
LIVERTON CL.
MOUNTAIN CL.
DOUGLAS CT.
SCARSDALE
ARDENNEY CT.
APPLEHAYES
MAER RD.
CRANFORD HO.
THE GABLES
PENTGROVE CT.

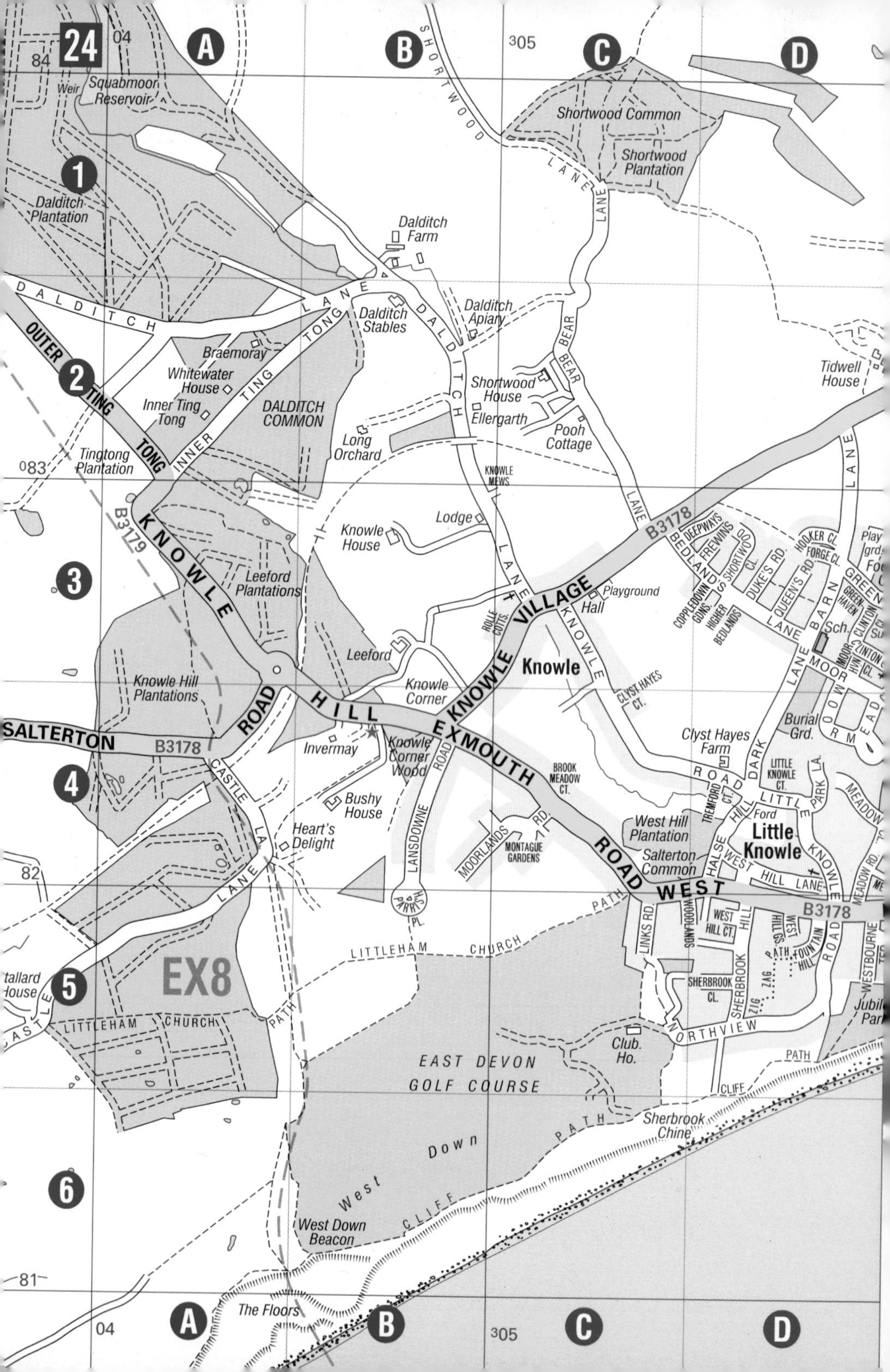

Squabmoor Reservoir
Weir
Dalditch Plantation
Dalditch Farm
Dalditch Stables
Dalditch Apiary
DALDITCH LANE
TING TONG
OUTER TING TONG
INNER TING TONG
Braemoray
Whitewater House
Inner Ting Tong
DALDITCH COMMON
Tingtong Plantation
SHORTWOOD LANE
Shortwood Common
Shortwood Plantation
BEAR LANE
Shortwood House
Ellergarth
Pooh Cottage
Long Orchard
KNOWLE MEWS
Lodge
Knowle House
Tidwell House
B3179
KNOWLE ROAD
Leeford Plantations
Knowle Hill Plantations
Leeford
Playground
Hall
Knowle
KNOWLE VILLAGE
ROLLE COTTS.
KNOWLE HILL
Knowle Corner
Knowle Corner Wood
Invermay
Bushy House
Heart's Delight
SALTERTON B3178
CASTLE LA.
CASTLE LANE
EXMOUTH ROAD WEST
LANSDOWNE ROAD
PARRISH PL.
BROOK MEADOW CT.
MOORLANDS RD.
MONTAGUE GARDENS
CLYST HAYES CT.
Clyst Hayes Farm
DEEPWAYS
FREWINS
BEDLANDS LANE
SHORTWOOD CL.
DUKE'S RD.
QUEEN'S RD.
HOOKER CL.
FORGE CL.
COPPLEDOWN GDNS.
HIGHER BEDLANDS
BARN LANE
GREEN HAVEN
CLINTON
Sch.
MOOR LANE
MEADOW
Burial Grd.
Play grds.
DARK LANE
TREMFORD CT.
LITTLE KNOWLE CT.
LITTLE PARK LA.
Ford
Little Knowle
West Hill Plantation
Salterton Common
HALSE HILL
WEST HILL LANE
KNOWLE ROAD
MEADOW RD.
B3178
LINKS RD.
WOODLANDS
WEST HILL CT.
SHERBROOK HILL
HILLS PATH
WEST FOUNTAIN HILL
ZIG ZAG PATH
SHERBROOK CL.
NORTHVIEW
WESTBOURNE
Jubilee Park
LITTLEHAM CHURCH PATH
EX8
Stallard House
EAST DEVON GOLF COURSE
Club Ho.
CLIFF PATH
Sherbrook Chine
West Down
West Down Beacon
The Floors
305
04
84
83
82
81
1
2
3
4
5
6
A
B
C
D

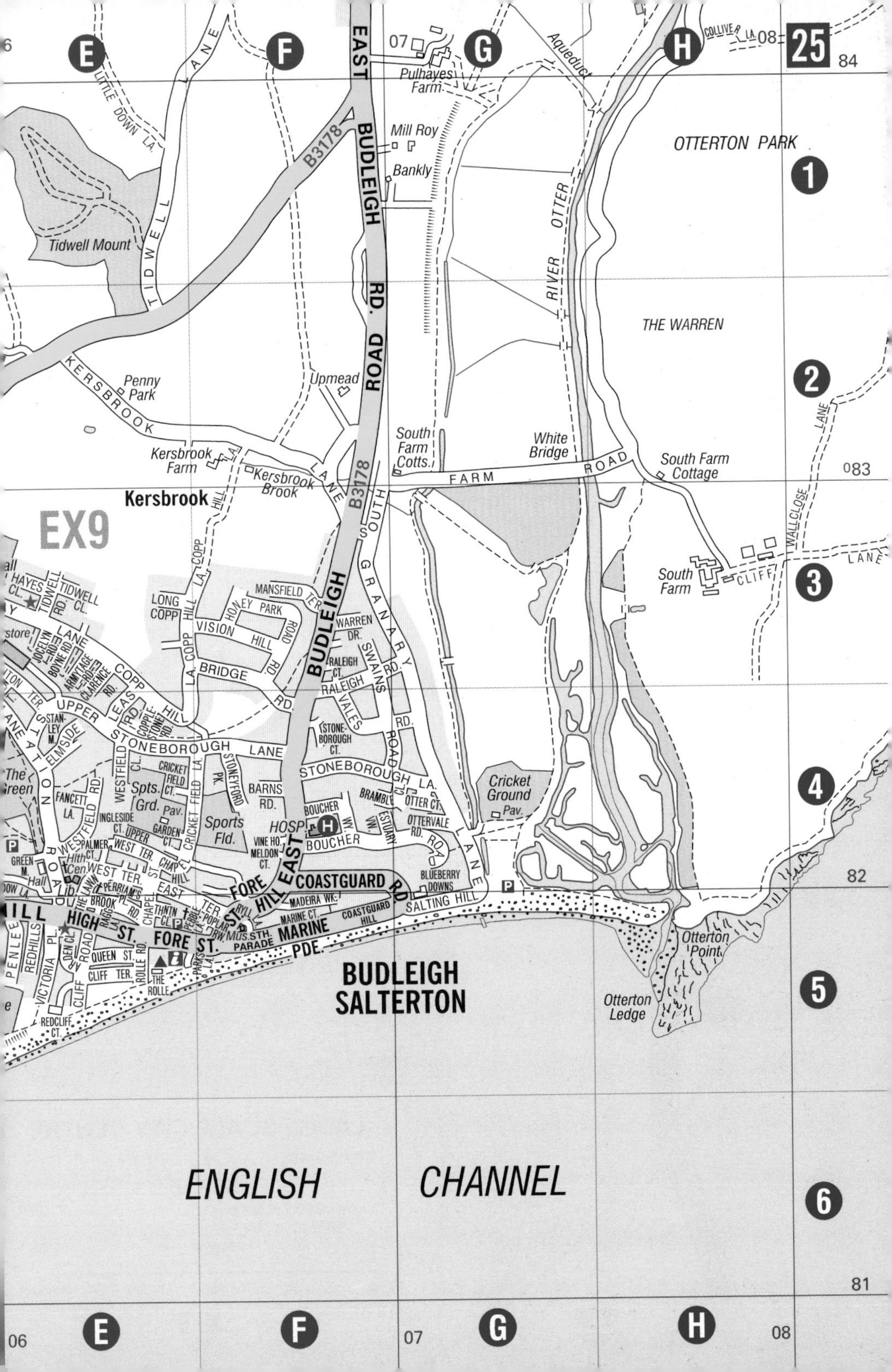

E
F
G
H
07
Pulhayes Farm
Aqueduct
COLLIVER LA.
08
84
LITTLE DOWN LA.
LANE
EAST BUDLEIGH ROAD
B3178
Mill Roy
Bankly
OTTERTON PARK
1
Tidwell Mount
TIDWELL
RIVER OTTER
THE WARREN
2
KERSBROOK
Penny Park
Upmead
South Farm Cotts.
White Bridge
FARM ROAD
South Farm Cottage
083
LANE
Kersbrook Farm
Kersbrook Brook
Kersbrook
EX9
WALLCLOSE
South Farm
CLIFF
LANE
3
HAYES CL.
TIDWELL RD.
TIDWELL CL.
LONG COPP
COPP HILL LA.
MANSFIELD TER.
HONEY PARK ROAD
VISION HILL
WARREN DR.
GRANARY
BRIDGE RD.
RALEIGH CT.
SWAINS RD.
RALEIGH RD.
VALES RD.
JOCELYN RD.
BOYNE RD.
ARMYTAGE RD.
CLARENCE RD.
COPP HILL
UPPER STONEBOROUGH LANE
LEAS RD.
STONE-BOROUGH CT.
STONEBOROUGH LA.
STATION ROAD
STANLEY M.
ELMSIDE
The Green
WESTFIELD CL.
CRICKET FIELD CT.
CRICKET FIELD LA.
STONEYFORD PK.
Spts. Grd.
Pav.
BARNS RD.
BRAMBLE CL.
OTTER CT.
Cricket Ground
Pav.
4
FANCETT LA.
WESTFIELD RD.
INGLESIDE CT.
UPPER WEST TER.
GARDEN CT.
Sports Fld.
HOSP.
BOUCHER WY.
BOUCHER RD.
VINE HO.
MELDON CT.
ESTUARY VW.
OTTERVALE RD.
ROAD
PALMER CT.
GREEN M.
Hall
Hlth. Cen.
WEST TER.
CHAPEL HILL
EAST TER.
FORE ST.
HILL
EAST
COASTGUARD RD.
BLUEBERRY DOWNS
LANE
P
82
PERRIAM'S PL.
BROOK RD.
MADEIRA WK.
SALTING HILL
Lib.
HIGH ST.
FORE ST.
THE LAWN
RAGG LA.
CHAPEL ST.
THNTN CL.
PEBBLE LA.
POPLAR RW.
RYLL LA.
Mus.
STH. PARADE
MARINE CT.
MARINE PDE.
COASTGUARD HILL
Otterton Point
PENLEE
REDHILLS
VICTORIA PL.
ARDEN CL.
ROAD
QUEEN ST.
ROLLE RD.
PARKS LA.
CLIFF TER.
THE ROLLE
CLIFF
REDCLIFF CT.
BUDLEIGH SALTERTON
Otterton Ledge
5
ENGLISH CHANNEL
6
81
06
07
08

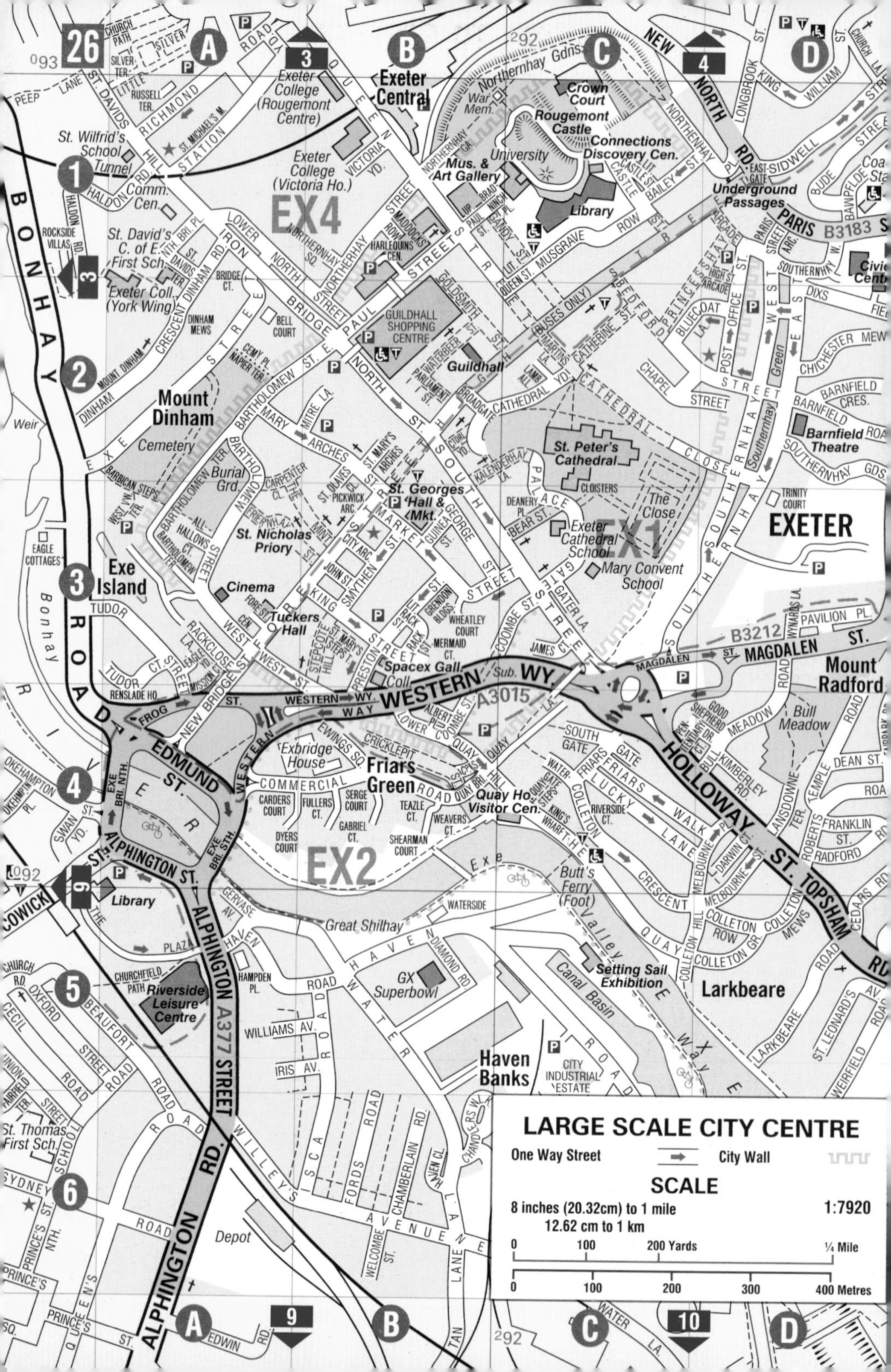
26
A
B
C
D
3
4
9
10
1
2
3
4
5
6
LARGE SCALE CITY CENTRE
One Way Street
City Wall
SCALE
8 inches (20.32cm) to 1 mile
1:7920
12.62 cm to 1 km
0
100
200 Yards
¼ Mile
0
100
200
300
400 Metres
EXETER
EX4
EX1
EX2
Exeter Central
Exeter College (Rougemont Centre)
Exeter College (Victoria Ho.)
Exeter Coll. (York Wing)
Crown Court
Rougemont Castle
Connections Discovery Cen.
University
Mus. & Art Gallery
Library
Underground Passages
Northernhay Gdns.
War Mem.
St. Wilfrid's School
Tunnel
Comm. Cen.
St. David's C. of E. First Sch.
Harlequins Cen.
Guildhall Shopping Centre
Guildhall
Mount Dinham
Cemetery
Burial Grd.
St. Nicholas Priory
St. Georges Hall & Mkt.
St. Peter's Cathedral
Cloisters
The Close
Exeter Cathedral School
Mary Convent School
Exe Island
Cinema
Tuckers Hall
Spacex Gall.
Coll.
Barnfield Theatre
Trinity Court
Mount Radford
Bull Meadow
Exbridge House
Friars Green
Quay Ho. Visitor Cen.
Butt's Ferry (Foot)
Great Shilhay
Waterside
GX Superbowl
Setting Sail Exhibition
Canal Basin
Larkbeare
Haven Banks
City Industrial Estate
Depot
Riverside Leisure Centre
Library
St. Thomas First Sch.
Eagle Cottages
Weir
Bonhay
Bonhay Road
Western Wy.
Western Way
A3015
B3212
B3183
A377
Alphington Street
Alphington Rd.
Alphington St.
Edmund St.
Frog St.
New Bridge St.
West St.
Commercial Road
Quay Hill
Magdalen St.
Holloway St.
Topsham Rd.
New North Rd.
Sidwell St.
Paris St.
Southernhay
Cathedral Close
South St.
North St.
High St.
Queen St.
Bedford St.
Fore St.
Bartholomew St. W.
Mary Arches St.
Smythen St.
King St.
Preston St.
Market St.
Coombe St.
Colleton Crescent
Friars Walk
Lucky Lane
Haven Road
Water Lane
Willeys Avenue
Cowick St.
Okehampton St.
Church Rd.
Oxford Road
Beaufort Road
Cecil Road
Sydney Rd.
Princes St.
Queens Rd.
Edwin Rd.
Tan Lane
Chamberlain Rd.
Fords Road
Welcombe St.
Haven Cl.
Chandlers Wk.
Williams Av.
Iris Av.
Hampden Pl.
Plaza
Gervase Av.
Larkbeare Rd.
St. Leonard's Av.
Weirfield Rd.
Lansdowne Ter.
Roberts Rd.
Franklin St.
Radford Rd.
Temple Rd.
Dean St.
Barnfield Cres.
Chichester Mews
Dixs Fields
Longbrook St.
King William St.
Bampfylde St.
Bude St.
Exe Valley Way
292
293
092
093

INDEX TO STREETS

Including Industrial Estates, selected Subsidiary Addresses, and selected Tourist Information.

HOW TO USE THIS INDEX

1. Each street name is followed by its Posttown or Postal Locality and then by its map reference;
   e.g. Abbeville Clo. *Exe* —3C **10** is in the Exeter Posttown and is to be found in square 3C on page **10**.
   The page number being shown in bold type.
   A strict alphabetical order is followed in which Av., Rd., St., etc. (though abbreviated) are read in full and as part of the street name; e.g. Applehayes appears after Apple Clo. but before Apple La.

2. Streets and a selection of Subsidiary names not shown on the Maps, appear in the index in *Italics* with the thoroughfare to which it is connected shown in brackets; e.g. *Albion Ct. Exm —3C **22** (off Union St.)*

GENERAL ABBREVIATIONS

All : Alley
App : Approach
Arc : Arcade
Av : Avenue
Bk : Back
Boulevd : Boulevard
Bri : Bridge
B'way : Broadway
Bldgs : Buildings
Bus : Business
Cvn : Caravan
Cen : Centre
Chu : Church
Chyd : Churchyard
Circ : Circle
Cir : Circus
Clo : Close
Comn : Common
Cotts : Cottages
Ct : Court
Cres : Crescent
Cft : Croft
Dri : Drive
E : East
VIII : Eighth
Embkmt : Embankment
Est : Estate
Fld : Field
V : Fifth
I : First
IV : Fourth
Gdns : Gardens
Gth : Garth
Ga : Gate
Gt : Great
Grn : Green
Gro : Grove
Ho : House
Ind : Industrial
Junct : Junction
La : Lane
Lit : Little
Lwr : Lower
Mc : Mac
Mnr : Manor
Mans : Mansions
Mkt : Market
Mdw : Meadow
M : Mews
Mt : Mount
N : North
Pal : Palace
Pde : Parade
Pk : Park
Pas : Passage
Pl : Place
Quad : Quadrant
Res : Residential
Ri : Rise
Rd : Road
St : Saint
II : Second
VII : Seventh
Shop : Shopping
VI : Sixth
S : South
Sq : Square
Sta : Station
St : Street
Ter : Terrace
III : Third
Trad : Trading
Up : Upper
Va : Vale
Vw : View
Vs : Villas
Wlk : Walk
W : West
Yd : Yard

POSTTOWN AND POSTAL LOCALITY ABBREVIATIONS

Alp : Alphington
Ayl : Aylesbeare
Bak H : Bakers Hill
Broad : Broadclyst
Bud : Budlake
Bud S : Budleigh Salterton
Bys : Bystock
Cly H : Clyst Honiton
Cly G : Clyst St George
Cly M : Clyst St Mary
Cow : Cowley
Ebf : Ebford
Exe : Exeter
Exe B : Exeter Bus. Pk.
Exmin : Exminster
Exm : Exmouth
Exo P : Exonia Park
Ext : Exton
Exw : Exwick
Hea : Heavitree
Ide : Ide
Kennf : Kennford
Kers : Kersbrook
Lit : Littleham
Long : Longdown
Lymp : Lympstone
Mar B : Marsh Barton Trad. Est.
Matf : Matford
Nadd : Nadderwater
Pin : Pinhoe
Ryd L : Rydon Lane
St Leo : St Leonards
St L : St Loyes
St T : St Thomas
Shi A : Shillingford Abbot
Shi S : Shillingford St George
Sow : Sowton
Sow I : Sowton Ind. Est.
Sto H : Stoke Hill
Top : Topsham
Whip : Whipton
White : Whitestone
Wood : Woodbury
Wood S : Woodbury Salterton

INDEX TO STREETS

Abbeville Clo. *Exe* —3C **10**
Abbey Ct. *Sow I* —1B **12**
Abbey Rd. *Exe* —4D **4**
Abbots Rd. *Exe* —4C **4**
Aboveway. *Exmin* —5B **16**
Acland Rd. *Exe* —5B **4**
Acland Ter. *Exe* —5A **4**
Adams Ter. *Exe* —1F **9**
Addison Clo. *Exe* —6E **3**
Admirals Wlk. *Exm* —5F **21**
A La Ronde. —4C **20**
Albany Clo. *Exm* —5G **21**
Alberta Cres. *Exe* —3D **4**
Albert Pl. *Exe* —1H **9** (4B **26**)
Albert Pl. *Exm* —3C **22**
Albert St. *Exe* —5B **4**
*Albion Ct. Exm —3C **22***
(off Union St.)
Albion Hill. *Exm* —2D **22**
Albion Pl. *Exe* —5B **4**
Albion Pl. *Exm* —3C **22**
Albion St. *Exe* —1G **9**
Albion St. *Exm* —2C **22**
Aldborough Ct. *Exm* —3E **23**
Aldens Grn. *Exe* —6H **9**
Aldens Rd. *Exe* —6H **9**
Aldrin Rd. *Exe* —2B **4**
Alexandra Ter. *Exe* —5C **4**
Alexandra Ter. *Exm* —3B **22**
Alexandra Wlk. *Exe* —1H **11**
Alford Clo. *Exe* —5G **5**
Alford Cres. *Exe* —5F **5**
Allervale Clo. *Exe* —2F **11**
Allhallows Ct. *Exe* —1H **9** (3A **26**)
Allington Mead. *Exe* —2G **3**
Alma Pl. *Exe* —1D **10**
Alpha Cen., The. *Sow I* —1B **12**
Alpha St. *Exe* —6D **4**
Alphin Brook Rd. *Mar B* —5H **9**
Alphington Rd. *Exe* —4H **9** (6A **26**)
Alphington Spur. *Exe* —5G **9**
Alphington St. *Exe* —1H **9** (4A **26**)
Altamira. *Top* —3F **17**
Ambassador Rd. *Exe B* —5A **6**
Amity Pl. *Top* —4F **17**
Anne Clo. *Exe* —3C **4**
Anson Rd. *Exm* —5E **21**
Anthony Rd. *Exe* —6D **4**
Antonine Cres. *Exe* —6E **3**
Apple Clo. *Exm* —4D **20**
Applehayes. *Exm* —4E **23**
Apple La. *Exe* —3A **12**
April Clo. *Exm* —4D **20**
Arcade. *Exe* —6A **4** (1D **26**)
Arch, The. *Wood* —5F **19**
Arcibald Rd. *Exe* —6B **4**
Arden Clo. *Bud S* —5E **25**
Ardenny Ct. *Exm* —4E **23**
Arena Pk. *Exe* —3F **5**
Argyll Rd. *Exe* —2G **3**
(in two parts)
Armstrong Av. *Exe* —2B **4**
Armytage Rd. *Bud S* —3E **25**
Arthurs Clo. *Exm* —5F **21**
Arthur's Rd. *Exe* —3E **5**
Arundel Clo. *Exe* —6H **9**
Ash Ct. *Shi S* —4A **14**
Ash Farm Clo. *Exe* —3B **6**
Ashfield Clo. *Exm* —6G **21**
Ashford Rd. *Top* —3E **17**
Ash Gro. *Exm* —5D **20**
Ash Leigh. *Alp* —6G **9**
Ashleigh Clo. *Exe* —6F **3**
Ashleigh Mt. Rd. *Exe* —6E **3**
Ashleigh Rd. *Exm* —2D **22**
Ashton Rd. *Mar B* —4H **9**
Ashwood Rd. *Exe* —3H **9**
Aspen Clo. *Exe* —2G **11**
Athelstan Rd. *Exe* —6B **4**
Atkinson Clo. *Exe* —3E **5**

Attwill's Almshouses. *Exe* —5G **3**
Attwyll Av. *Exe* —1E **11**
Austin Clo. *Exe* —4G **5**
Avalon Clo. *Exe* —2E **5**
Avocet Rd. *Sow I* —6B **6**
Avondale Rd. *Exe* —1E **11**
Avondale Rd. *Exm* —1F **23**

Badger Clo. *Exe* —1H **11**
Bad Homburg Way. *Mar B* —6B **10**
Badon Clo. *Exe* —2E **5**
Bagshot Av. *Exe* —3B **10**
Bailey St. *Exe* —6A **4** (1C **26**)
Baker Pl. *Exe* —1F **11**
Baker St. *Exe* —1D **10**
Bakery La. *Exm* —2C **22**
Ballard Ct. *Exm* —6G **21**
Ball's Farm. *Ide* —4E **9**
Balmoral Gdns. *Top* —3F **17**
Bampfylde St. *Exe* —6A **4** (1D **26**)
Bankside. *Exm* —4E **21**
Bapton Clo. *Exm* —5D **20**
Bapton La. *Exm* —6D **20** (in two parts)
Barbican Steps. *Exe* —6H **3** (2A **26**)
Baring Cres. *Exe* —6C **4**
Baring Ter. *Exe* —2A **10**
Barley Farm Rd. *Exe* —2E **9**
Barley La. *Exe* —6D **2**
Barley Mt. *Exe* —1E **9**
Barnardo Rd. *Exe* —2A **10**
Barnfield Av. *Exm* —2F **23**
Barnfield Cres. *Exe* —6A **4** (2D **26**)
Barnfield Hill. *Exe* —6B **4**
Barnfield Rd. *Exe* —6A **4** (2D **26**)
Barn La. *Bud S* —3D **24**
Barns Rd. *Bud S* —4F **25**
Barnstone Ct. *Exe* —6G **9**
Barrack La. *Shi A* —2C **14**
Barrack Rd. *Exe* —1C **10**
Barrowdale Clo. *Exm* —4E **21**
Bartholomew St. E. *Exe* —6H **3** (2A **26**)
Bartholomew St. W. *Exe* —1H **9** (2A **26**)
Bartholomew Ter. *Exe* —1H **9** (3A **26**)
Bartlett Mt. *Exe* —1B **10**
Barton Clo. *Ext* —6A **18**
Barton Ct. *Exe* —5G **5**
Barton La. *Shi A* —2A **14**
Barton Rd. *Exe* —2F **9**
Bassetts Gdns. *Exm* —5F **21**
Bath Rd. *Exm* —3C **22**
Baxter Clo. *Exe* —3H **11**
Bazley Sq. *Exe* —4A **6**
Beacon Av. *Exe* —4D **4** (in two parts)
Beacon Heath. *Exe* —3F **5**
Beacon Hill. *Exm* —3C **22**
Beacon La. *Exe* —3E **5**
Beacon Pl. *Exm* —3C **22**
Beacon, The. *Exm* —3C **22**
Bear La. *Bud S* —2C **24**
Bear St. *Exe* —1A **10** (3C **26**)
Beaufort Rd. *Exe* —2G **9** (5A **26**)
Beaworthy Clo. *Exe* —4G **9**
Beck Cft. *Exe* —6D **4**
Bedford St. *Exe* —6A **4** (2C **26**)
Bedland's La. *Bud S* —3C **24**
Beech Av. *Exe* —3B **4**
Beeches Clo. *Wood* —6F **19**
Beechway. *Exm* —1D **22**
Bees Ter. *Kennf* —6C **14**
Belgrave Rd. *Exe* —6B **4**
Bell Ct. *Exe* —6H **3** (2A **26**)
Belle Vue Rd. *Exe* —2G **3** (in two parts)
Belle Vue Rd. *Exm* —1C **22**
Belmont Rd. *Exe* —5B **4**
Belmont Ter. *Exm* —6E **21**
Belvedere Clo. *Top* —2E **17**
Belvedere Rd. *Exm* —2C **22**
Belvidere Rd. *Exe* —3G **3**
Bennett Clo. *Exe* —6G **9**
Bennett Sq. *Exe* —4E **5**
Berkshire Dri. *Exe* —2E **9**
Bernadette Clo. *Exe* —3G **5**
Berrybrook Mdw. *Exmin* —5B **16**
Berry Clo. *Exm* —1G **23**
Betony Ri. *Exe* —3G **11**
Bettysmead. *Exe* —3E **5**
Bettysmead Ct. *Exe* —4E **5**
Beverley Clo. *Exe* —2F **11**
Bicton Pl. *Exe* —6D **4**
Bicton Pl. *Exm* —3C **22**
Bicton St. *Exm* —3C **22**
Bicton Vs. *Exm* —3D **22**
Bidmead Clo. *Exm* —2G **23**
Bindon Rd. *Exe* —2A **6**
Binford Clo. *Exe* —6F **5**
Birch Rd. *Lymp* —2A **20**
Birchwood Rd. *Exm* —5F **21**
Birchy Barton Hill. *Exe* —1F **11**
Birdspring Wlk. *Exe* —3D **4**
Birkett Clo. *Exe* —2G **11**
Bishop Ct. Quarry. *Exe* —2A **12**
Bishops Ct. Ind. Est. *Exe* —2A **12**
Bishop's Ct. La. *Cly M* —3D **12**
Bishop Westall Rd. *Exe* —4E **11**
Bittern Rd. *Sow I* —6A **6**
Blackall Rd. *Exe* —5A **4**
Black Boy Rd. *Exe* —5B **4**
Black Hat La. *Long* —3A **8**
Blackhorse La. *Exe* —4C **6**
Blackmore Ct. *Exm* —6G **21**
Blackthorn Cres. *Exe* —6G **5**
Blenheim Ct. Exe —5A 10 (off Lustleigh Clo.)
Blenheim Rd. *Exe* —4H **9**
Blueberry Downs. *Bud S* —5G **25**
Blue Cedar Ct. *Exm* —3D **22**
Bluecoat La. *Exe* —6A **4** (2C **26**)
Bluehayes La. *Broad* —1H **7**
Boarden Barn. *Exm* —3D **22**
Bodley Clo. *Exe* —5F **5**
Bodley Ho. *Exe* —5F **5**
Bond's La. *Wood S* —4E **19**
Bonfire La. *Wood* —5F **19**
Bonhay Rd. *Exe* —5G **3** (1A **26**)
Bonnington Gro. *Exe* —6D **4**
Bonville Clo. *Exe* —5F **5**
Booth Way. *Exm* —5D **20**
Boucher Rd. *Bud S* —4F **25**
Boucher Way. *Bud S* —4F **25**
Bourn Ri. *Exe* —2H **5**
Bovemoor's La. *Exe* —1D **10**
Bowhay La. *Exe* —1E **9**
Bowling Green Marsh Nature Reserve. —4G **17**
Bowling Grn. Rd. *Top* —4G **17**
Bowring Clo. *Exe* —5F **5**
Boyne Rd. *Bud S* —3E **25**
Brackendale. *Exm* —3E **21**
Brackenwood. *Exm* —6E **21**
Bradfield Rd. *Exe* —3H **5**
Bradford Clo. *Exm* —4E **21**
Bradham Ct. *Exm* —1F **23**
Bradham La. *Exm* —1F **23**
Bradninch Pl. *Exe* —6H **3** (1B **26**)
Bramble Clo. *Bud S* —4F **25**
Bramley Av. *Exe* —6G **5**
Branscombe Clo. *Exe* —1E **9**
Brent Clo. *Wood* —5G **19**
Brenton Rd. *Kennf* —6A **14**
Brentor Clo. *Exe* —4F **3**
Breton Way. *Exm* —6G **21**
Bretteville Clo. *Wood* —5G **19**
Briar Av. *Exe* —4D **10**
Briar Clo. *Exm* —1F **23**
Brickleigh Clo. *Exe* —2H **5**
Bridford Rd. *Mar B* —4A **10**
Bridge Cotts. *Exe* —4B **4**
Bridge Ct. *Exe* —2A **26**
Bridge Hill. *Top* —3F **17**
Bridgehill Gth. *Top* —3F **17**
Bridge Rd. *Bud S* —3F **25**
Bridge Rd. *Exmin* —1H **15**
Bridge Rd. *Exm* —1C **22**
Bridges Av. *Exm* —4E **21**
Bridspring Rd. *Exe* —3D **4**
Brimpenny Rd. *Exm* —6E **21**
Brittany Rd. *Exm* —4E **21**
Britten Dri. *Exe* —1F **11**
Brixington Dri. *Exm* —5F **21**
Brixington La. *Exm* —6E **21** (in two parts)
Broadfields Rd. *Exe* —1G **11**
Broadgate. *Exe* —6H **3** (2B **26**)
Broadleaf Clo. *Exe* —4A **6**
Broadmead. *Exm* —5F **21**
Broadmead. *Wood* —5F **19**
Broadmeadow Av. *Exe* —2F **9**
Broad Pk. Rd. *Exm* —6E **21**
Broadparks Av. *Exe* —2A **6**
Broadparks Clo. *Exe* —2A **6**
Brookway. *Exe* —5F **5**
Broadway. *Exe* —3F **9**
Broadway. *Wood* —6F **19**
Broadway Hill. *Exe* —3E **9**
Broadway, The. *Exm* —1G **23**
Brodick Clo. *Exe* —3B **4**
Brook Clo. *Exe* —4F **5**
Brooke Av. *Exe* —3D **10**
Brookfield Gdns. *Exe* —5H **9**
Brook Grn. Ter. *Exe* —5B **4**
Brookhayes Clo. *Exm* —1D **22**
Brooklands Rd. *Exm* —6F **21**
Brookleigh Av. *Exe* —1F **11**
Brooklyn Pk. *Exm* —6E **21**
Brook Mdw. *Exm* —6E **21**
Brook Mdw. Ct. *Bud S* —4C **24**
Brook Rd. *Bud S* —5E **25**
Brookside Cres. *Exe* —2F **5**
Broom Clo. *Exe* —1E **11**
Brownlees. *Exmin* —4A **16**
Brownling Clo. *Exe* —2E **11**
Brunswick St. *Exe* —1G **9**
Bryon Way. *Exm* —4E **21**
Buckerell Av. *Exe* —3C **10**
Buckingham Clo. *Exm* —2G **23**
Bucknill Clo. *Exmin* —4A **16**
Buddle La. *Exe* —1F **9**
Bude St. *Exe* —6A **4** (1D **26**)
Budlake Rd. *Mar B* —5A **10**
Buller Rd. *Exe* —1G **9**
Bull Mdw. Rd. *Exe* —1A **10** (4D **26**)
Bungalow La. *Exe* —2B **10**
Bunn Rd. *Exm* —3F **21**
Burch Clo. *Exm* —5G **21**
Burgmanns Hill. *Lymp* —2A **20**
Burnet Clo. *Exe* —3G **11**
Burns Av. *Exe* —3D **10**
Burnside. *Exm* —6D **20**
Burnthouse La. *Exe* —3D **10**
Burrator Dri. *Exe* —5E **3**
Butts Rd. *Exe* —1E **11**
Byron Rd. *Exe* —1G **11**
Bystock Clo. *Exe* —5H **3** (1A **26**)
Bystock M. *Bys* —4G **21**
Bystock Rd. *Exm* —3F **21**
Bystock Ter. *Exe* —5H **3** (1A **26**)

California Clo. *Exe* —1B **4**
Calthorpe Rd. *Exe* —4D **4**
Cambridge St. *Exe* —1G **9**
Camelot Clo. *Exe* —3E **5**
Camperdown Ter. *Exm* —3A **22**
Campion Gdns. *Exe* —3F **11**
Canal Banks. *Exe* —3A **10**
Canberra Clo. *Exe* —2C **4**
Candy's Path. *Lymp* —2A **20**
Canon Way. *Exe* —6H **9**
Canterbury Rd. *Exe* —5E **3**
Canterbury Way. *Exm* —3G **21**
Capel Cotts. *Exm* —2H **23**
Capel La. *Exm* —1H **23**
Carberry Av. *Exm* —6C **20**
Carders Ct. *Exe* —1H **9** (4A **26**)
Carlile Rd. *Exe* —1E **11**
Carlton Hill. *Exm* —4C **22**
Carlton Rd. *Exe* —2F **11**
Carlyon Clo. *Exe* —6E **5**
Carlyon Gdns. *Exe* —6E **5**
Caroline Clo. *Exm* —6F **21**
Carpenter Clo. *Exe* —1H **9**
Carter Av. *Exm* —1C **22**
Castle La. *Exm* —2H **23** (in two parts)
Castle La. *Wood* —5G **19**

Castle St. *Exe* —6A **4** (1C **26**)
Cathedral Clo. *Exe* —6A **4** (2C **26**)
Cathedral Yd. *Exe* (in two parts) —6A **4** (2B **26**)
Catherine St. *Exe* —6A **4** (2C **26**)
Cauleston Clo. *Exm* —5C **20**
Causey Gdns. *Exe* —3B **6**
Causey La. *Exe* —3B **6**
Cavendish Rd. *Exe* —6D **4**
Cecil Rd. *Exe* —2G **9** (5A **26**)
Cedar Clo. *Exm* —4F **21**
Cedars Rd. *Exe* —2A **10** (5D **26**)
Celia Cres. *Exe* —2E **5**
Cemetery Pl. *Exe* —6H **3** (2A **26**)
Central Av. *Exe* —1D **16** (EX2)
Central Av. *Exe* —2F **5** (EX4)
Chamberlain Rd. *Exe* —2H **9** (6B **26**)
Chancel Ct. *Exe* —3H **5**
Chancel La. *Exe* —3H **5**
Chancellor's Way. *Exe* —2E **5**
Chandlers Wlk. *Exe* —2H **9** (6B **26**)
Chantry Mdw. *Exe* —6H **9**
Chapel Hill. *Bud S* —4E **25**
Chapel Hill. *Exm* —3C **22**
Chapel Pl. *Top* —3F **17**
Chapel Rd. *Exe* —5H **9**
Chapel Rd. *Lymp* —2A **20**
Chapel St. *Bud S* —5E **25**
Chapel St. *Exe* —6A **4** (2C **26**)
Chard Rd. *Exe* —6E **5**
Chardstock Clo. *Exe* —6H **5**
Charingthay Ga. *Exe* —4C **4**
Charles St. *Exm* —2C **22**
Charney Av. *Exe* —1E **9**
Chatham Clo. *Exm* —6F **21**
Chaucer Av. *Exe* —3D **10**
Cheeke St. *Exe* —6B **4**
Chelmsford Rd. *Exe* —6D **2**
Cheltenham Clo. *Exe* —5E **3**
Chepstowe Clo. *Exe* —6F **11**
Cheriswood Av. *Exm* —6F **21**
Cheriswood Clo. *Exm* —6F **21**
Cherry Clo. *Exm* —4E **21**
Cherry Gdns. *Exe* —2E **11**
Cherry Tree Clo. *Exe* —1G **3**
Cheshire Rd. *Exm* —5G **21**
Chester Clo. *Exe* —5E **3**
Chestnut Av. *Exe* —3E **11**
Chestnut Clo. *Exm* —4E **21**
Chestnut Ct. *Exe* —6H **9**
Cheynegate La. *Exe* —1G **5**
Cheyne Ri. *Exe* —2H **5**
Chichester Clo. *Exm* —2E **23**
Chichester Ho. *Exe* —1F **11**
Chichester M. *Exe* —6A **4** (2D **26**)
Christow Rd. *Mar B* —4H **9**
Chudleigh Rd. *Exe* —6H **9**
Chudley Clo. *Exm* —6F **21**
Churchfield Path. *Exe* —2H **9** (5A **26**) (nr. Beaufort Rd.)
Churchfield Path. *Exe* —2G **9** (nr. Church Rd.)
Church Hill. *Pin* —1G **5**
Churchill Ct. *Lymp* —1A **20**
Churchill Rd. *Exe* —2F **9**
Churchill Rd. *Exm* —5F **21**
Church La. *Cly M* —4D **12**
Church La. *Exe* —5A **4** (1D **26**)
Church La. *Hea* —1D **10**
Church La. *Pin* —2H **5**
Church La. *St T* —2G **9**
Church Path. *Exe* —5H **3** (1A **26**)
Church Path. *Top* —3F **17**
Chu. Path La. *Hea* —1E **11**
Churchpath Rd. *Exe* —3F **9**
Church Rd. *Alp* —4H **9**
Church Rd. *Exm* —2C **22**
Church Rd. *Lymp* —2A **20**
Church Rd. *St T* —2G **9** (5A **26**)
Churchside. *Cly H* —5F **7**
Churchstile. *Exmin* —4B **16**
Church Stile La. *Wood* —5F **19**
Church St. *Exm* —3C **22**
Church St. *Hea* —1D **10**
Church Ter. *Exe* —1D **10**
Chute St. *Exe* —5B **4**
City Arc. *Exe* —1H **9** (3B **26**)
City Ind. Est. *Exe* —2A **10**
Clapperbrook La. *Exe* —5H **9**
Clara Pl. *Top* —3E **17**
Claredale Rd. *Exm* —3D **22**
Claremont Gro. *Exe* —2B **10**
Claremont Gro. *Exm* —2D **22**
Claremont La. *Exm* —2E **23**
Clarence Pl. *Exe* —5B **4**
Clarence Rd. *Bud S* —4E **25**
Clarence Rd. *Exe* —1G **9**
Clarence Rd. *Exm* —2C **22**
Clarke Mead. *Exe* —2G **11**
Clay La. *Exm* —3A **20**
Clayton Rd. *Exe* —5G **3**
Clerk Clo. *Exm* —5E **21**
Clevedon Clo. *Exe* —3B **4**
Cleveland Ct. *Exe* —5B **4**
Cleveland Pl. *Exm* —3B **22**
Cleveland St. *Exe* —1G **9**
Cleve Rd. *Exe* —6F **3**
Cliff Baston Clo. *Exe* —2G **11**
Cliff La. *Bud S* —3H **25**
Clifford Clo. *Exe* —5F **5**
Clifford Rd. *Exe* —4D **4**
Cliff Path. *Bud S* —6B **24**
Cliff Rd. *Bud S* —5E **25**
Cliff Ter. *Bud S* —5E **25**
Clifton Hill. *Exe* —5C **4**
Clifton Rd. *Exe* —6B **4**
Clifton St. *Exe* —6B **4**
Clinton Av. *Exe* —4C **4**
Clinton Clo. *Bud S* —3D **24**
Clinton Sq. *Exm* —3B **22**
Clinton St. *Exe* —1G **9**
Clinton Ter. *Bud S* —3E **25**
Cliston Av. *Exm* —5F **21**
Cloister Rd. *Exe* —4D **4**
Cloisters. *Exe* —6A **4** (3C **26**)
Cluden Clo. *Exe* —6H **9**
Clydesdale Rd. *Exe* —3G **3**
Clyst Halt Av. *Exe* —3A **12**
Clyst Hayes Ct. *Bud S* —4C **24**
Clyst Heath. *Exe* —3H **11**
Clystide. *Cly H* —4F **7**
Clyst Rd. *Top* —1E **17**
Clyst Valley. *Cly M* —4D **12**
Coastguard Hill. *Bud S* —5F **25**
Coastguard Rd. *Bud S* —4F **25**
Coates Rd. *Exe* —1F **11**
Codrington St. *Exe* —6B **4**
Coffins La. *Exmin* —5H **15**
Cofton Rd. *Mar B* —5B **10**
Colands Ct. *Exe* —6G **9**
Coleridge Clo. *Exm* —3E **21**
Coleridge Rd. *Exe* —2F **9**
College Av. *Exe* —1B **10**
College La. *Ide* —4C **8**
College Rd. *Exe* —1B **10**
College, The. *Ide* —4D **8**
Colleton Clo. *Exm* —1E **23**
Colleton Cres. *Exe* —1A **10**
Colleton Gro. *Exe* —2A **10** (5D **26**)
Colleton Hill. *Exe* —2A **10** (5C **26**)
Colleton M. *Exe* —2A **10** (5D **26**)
Colleton Row. *Exe* —2A **10** (5D **26**)
Colleton Way. *Exm* —1E **23**
Collins La. *Exe* —2B **4**
Colliver La. *Bud S* —1H **25**
Colvin Clo. *Exm* —2F **23**
Comilla Clo. *Exm* —4E **21**
Commercial Rd. *Exe* —1H **9** (4A **26**)
Commin's Rd. *Exe* —5D **4**
Concorde Rd. *Exm* —6G **21**
Connections Discovery Centre. —6A **4** (1C **26**)
Conrad Av. *Exe* —4F **5**
Conybeare Clo. *Exe* —5E **5**
Cook Sq. *Exmin* —5B **16**
Coombe St. *Exe* —1A **10** (3C **26**)
Copperfield Clo. *Exm* —6G **21**
Copp Hill La. *Bud S* —3E **25** (in two parts)
Coppledown Gdns. *Bud S* —3C **24**
Copplestone Rd. *Bud S* —4E **25**
Copse. *Exm* —5G **21**
Copse, The. *Exe* —1C **16**
Cordery Rd. *Exe* —3F **9**
Cornflower Hill. *Exe* —4D **2**
Cornmill Cres. *Exe* —5G **9**
Cornwall St. *Exe* —1G **9**
Coronation Rd. *Exe* —2E **11**
Cotfield St. *Exe* —3A **10**
Cotterell Clo. *Broad* —2G **7**
Cottey Cres. *Exe* —2E **5**
Cottles La. *Wood* —4G **19**
Countess Wear Rd. *Exe* —5E **11**
Couper Meadows. *Exe* —3H **11**
Courtenay Gdns. *Alp* —6G **9**
Courtenay Rd. *Exe* —3H **9**
Courtlands La. *Exm* —3B **20**
Coventry Rd. *Exe* —6F **3**
Coverdale Rd. *Exe* —3H **9**
Cowick Hill. *Exe* —3E **9**
Cowick La. *Exe* —4G **9**
Cowick Rd. *Exe* —2G **9**
Cowick St. *Exe* —2F **9** (5A **26**)
Cowley Bri. Rd. *Exe* —1F **3**
Cowper Av. *Exe* —3C **10**
Crabb La. *Exe* —4G **9**
Craig Cotts. *Cly M* —3C **12**
Cranbrook Rd. *Exe* —1E **11**
Cranford Av. *Exm* —3E **23**
Cranford Clo. *Exm* —3E **23**
Cranford Ho. *Exm* —3F **23**
Cranford Vw. *Exm* —3E **23**
Cranmere Ct. *Exe* —5A **10**
Crawford Gdns. *Exe* —3G **9**
Creadly La. *Top* —2F **17**
Crealy Farm Park. —4H **13**
Crediton Rd. *Cow* —1F **3**
Creely Clo. *Exe* —6A **10**
Crescent, The. *Exm* —1G **23**
Cricketfield Ct. *Bud S* —4E **25**
Cricket Fld. La. *Bud S* —4E **25**
Cricklepit St. *Exe* —1H **9** (4B **26**)
Critchards. *Wood* —6G **19**
Criterion Pl. Exm —3C 22 (off High St. Exmouth,)
Crockwells Clo. *Exmin* —5B **16**
Crockwells Rd. *Exmin* —5B **16**
Croft Chase. *Exe* —2E **9**
Cromwell Ct. *Exe* —1E **11**
Crossingfields Dri. *Exm* —6C **20**
Crossmead Vs. *Exe* —3D **8**
Cross Vw. *Exe* —5H **9**
Cross Vw. Ter. *Ide* —4E **9**
Crowder's Hill. *Exm* —4D **20**
Crudges La. *Exm* —2C **22**
Culverland Clo. *Exe* —4B **4**
Culverland Rd. *Exe* —4B **4**
Culvery Clo. *Wood* —5G **19**
Cumberland Ct. *Exm* —6F **21**
Cunningham Rd. *Exm* —5F **21**
Curlew Way. *Exe* —2A **4**
Cutteridge La. *White* —1A **8**
Cygnet Ind. Units. *Sow I* —1A **12**
Cypress Dri. *Exe* —5F **3**
Cyprus Rd. *Exm* —3D **22**

Dagmar Rd. *Exm* —3C **22**
Dairy Clo. *Exmin* —5B **16**
Daisy Links. *Exe* —4D **2**
Dalditch La. *Bud S* —2A **24**
Daleside Rd. *Exe* —3C **4**
Danby La. *Exm* —2C **22**
Danby Ter. *Exm* —2C **22**
Danes Rd. *Exe* —5H **3**
Danesway. *Exe* —2A **6**
Dark La. *Bud S* —4D **24**
Dark La. *Exmin* —6H **15**
Darwin Ct. *Exe* —1A **10** (4D **26**)
Dawlish Pk. Ter. *Exm* —3B **20**
Dawlish Rd. *Exe* —6H **9**
Dawlish Rd. *Exmin* —1G **15**
Dawn Clo. *Exe* —6E **5**
Days-Pottles La. *Exmin* —4E **15**

Deacon Clo. *Exe* —6H **9**
Deanery Pl. Exe —3C ***26*** *(off South St.)*
Dean St. *Exe* —1A **10** (4D **26**)
Deepdene Pk. *Exe* —2C **10**
Deepway Ct. *Exmin* —4A **16**
Deepway Gdns. *Exmin* —4H **15**
Deepway La. *Matf* —3F **15** (in two parts)
Deepways. *Bud S* —3C **24**
De La Rue Way. *Exe* —3H **5**
Delderfield Gdns. *Exm* —3E **23**
Delius Cres. *Exe* —1G **11**
Dene Clo. *Exm* —6F **21**
Dening Ct. *Exm* —1D **22**
Denise Clo. *Exe* —6H **9**
Denmark Rd. *Exe* —1B **10**
Denmark Rd. *Exm* —1F **23**
Denver Clo. *Top* —2E **17**
Denver Rd. *Top* —2E **17**
Devon County Showground. (Westpoint) —3F **13**
Devon Rd. *Exe* —4D **4**
Devonshire Pl. *Exe* —4B **4**
Devonshire Regimental Museum. —3C **10**
Diamond Rd. *Exe* —2H **9** (5B **26**)
Diane Clo. *Exm* —3F **21**
Dickens Dri. *Exe* —3D **10**
Dick Pym Clo. *Exe* —2G **11**
Digby Dri. *Exe* —3H **11**
Digby Ho. *Exe* —3H **11**
Dinan Way. *Exm* —3E **21**
Dinham Cres. *Exe* —6H **3** (2A **26**)
Dinham M. *Exe* —2A **26**
Dinham Rd. *Exe* —6H **3** (2A **26**)
Dix's Fld. *Exe* —6A **4** (2D **26**)
Dock Rd. *Exm* —3A **22**
Doctors Wlk. *Exe* —3D **8** (in two parts)
Dorchester Way. *Exm* —3F **21**
Doriam Clo. *Exe* —2A **4**
Dorset Av. *Exe* —2E **9**
Dotton Clo. *Exe* —6H **5**
Douglas Av. *Exm* —4D **22**
Douglas Ct. *Exm* —3E **23**
Dove Way. *Exo P* —3D **8**
Drake Av. *Exe* —1H **11**
Drake's Av. *Exm* —1F **23**
Drakes Farm. *Ide* —4E **9**
Drakes Gdns. *Exm* —1F **23**
Drakes Rd. *Exe* —2G **9**
Draycott Clo. *Exe* —2E **11**
Dryden Rd. *Exe* —2D **10**
Dryfield. *Exmin* —4B **16**
Duckworth Rd. *Exe* —3G **9**
Duke of Cornwall Clo. *Exm* —6G **21**
Dukes Cres. *Exm* —6G **21**
Duke's Rd. *Bud S* —3D **24**
Dunchideock Rd. *Exe* —6D **8**
Dunrich Clo. *Exe* —1B **10**
Dunsford Clo. *Exm* —3F **23**
Dunsford Gdns. *Exe* —3E **9**
Dunsford Rd. *Exe* —3D **8**
Dunvegan Clo. *Exe* —4G **3**
Durham Clo. *Exe* —5G **5**
Durham Clo. *Exm* —3F **21**
Dutch Ct. *Top* —4F **17**
Dyers Ct. *Exe* —1H **9** (4A **26**)

Eager Way. *Exmin* —3H **15**
Eagle Cotts. *Exe* —1G **9**
Eagles Nest. *Exe* —2D **8**
Eagle Way. *Sow I* —2B **12**
Eagle Yd. *Exe* —3A **26**
Earl Richards Rd. N. *Exe* —3C **10**
Earl Richards Rd. S. *Exe* —4D **10**
East Av. *Exe* —5C **4**
E. Budleigh Rd. *Bud S* —1F **25**
East Dri. *Exm* —6C **20**
Eastern Av. *Exe* —1C **16**
Eastgate. *Exe* —6A **4** (1D **26**)
E. Grove Rd. *Exe* —2B **10**
E. John Wlk. *Exe* —6C **4**
East Ter. *Bud S* —4E **25**
East Ter. *Exe* —6E **5**
E. View Ter. *Exe* —4B **4**
E. Wonford Hill. *Exe* —1E **11**
Eaton Dri. *Exe* —6B **4**
Ebford La. *Ebf* —4A **18**
Ebrington Rd. *Exe* —3H **9**
Edgebaston Mead. *Exe* —2G **11**
Edgerton Pk. Rd. *Exe* —4B **4**
Edinburgh Cres. *Lymp* —1A **20**
Edinburgh Dri. *Exe* —6E **3**
Edmonton Clo. *Exe* —4E **5**
Edmund St. *Exe* —1H **9** (4A **26**)
Edwin Rd. *Exe* —3H **9** (6A **26**)
Egham Av. *Exe* —3B **10**
Egremont Rd. *Exm* —1C **22**
Elaine Clo. *Exe* —3E **5**
Eldertree Gdns. *Exe* —5G **3**
Elgar Clo. *Exe* —1G **11**
Elizabeth Av. *Exe* —4C **4**
Elizabeth Rd. *Exm* —5E **21**
Ellards Clo. *Exe* —3C **10**
Elliott Clo. *Exe* —2C **4**
Ellwood Rd. *Exm* —5F **21**
Elmbridge Gdns. *Exe* —4G **3**
Elmbrook. *Exe* —5H **3**
Elmdon Clo. *Exe* —3B **4**
Elmfield Cres. *Exm* —5C **20**
Elm Gro. *Exe* —5H **3**
Elm Gro. *Exm* —3B **22**
Elm Gro. Av. *Top* —3F **17**
Elm Gro. Gdns. *Top* —3F **17**
Elm Gro. Rd. *Top* —3F **17**
Elm La. *Exm* —2H **23**
Elm Rd. *Exm* —2E **23**
Elmside. *Bud S* —4E **25**
Elmside. *Exe* —5C **4**
Elmside Clo. *Exe* —5C **4**
Elton Rd. *Exe* —4C **4**
Elvis Rd. *Exm* —2F **23**
Elwyn Rd. *Exm* —2E **23**
Ely Clo. *Exe* —6D **2**
Emardon Hill. *Exe* —3H **3**
Emmanuel Ct. *Exe* —1G **9**
Emmanuel Rd. *Exe* —1G **9**
Emmnsfield. *Exm* —2F **23**
Emperor Way. *Exe B* —6A **6**
Endfield Clo. *Exe* —6F **5**
Endsleigh Cres. *Cly H* —5D **6**
Ennerdale Wlk. *Exe* —6F **3**
Esplanade. *Exm* —3B **22**
Essex Clo. *Exe* —3E **9**
Essington Clo. *Exm* —4D **20**
Essington Ct. *Exm* —4D **20**
Estuary Ct. *Exm* —3A **22**
Estuary Vw. *Bud S* —4F **25**
Etonhurst Clo. *Exe* —3H **11**
Evans Cotts. *Bud S* —4D **24**
Everall Vs. *Lymp* —1A **20**
Evergreen Clo. *Exm* —4F **21**
Evert Clo. *Exm* —1G **23**
Ewings Sq. *Exe* —1H **9** (4B **26**)
Excalibur Clo. *Exe* —3E **5**
Exe Bri. N. *Exe* —1H **9** (4A **26**)
Exe Bri. S. *Exe* —1H **9** (4A **26**)
Exe St. *Exe* —6H **3** (2A **26**)
Exe St. *Top* —3F **17**
Exeter Bus. Pk. *Exe* —5A **6**
Exeter Guildhall. —2C **26**
Exeter Rd. *Exe* —1D **16**
Exeter Rd. *Exm* —4C **20**
Exe Va. Rd. *Exe* —5E **11**
Exe Vw. Cotts. *Exe* —4F **3**
Exe Vw. Rd. *Lymp* —1D **20**
Exhibition Way. *Exe* —3G **5**
Exminster Marshes Bird Sanctuary. —5D **16**
Exminster Hill. *Exmin* —6A **16**
Exmouth Ct. *Exm* —3D **22**
Exmouth Express. (Miniature Railway) —4C **22**
Exmouth Lifeboat Station. —4C **22**
Exmouth Museum. —2C **22**
Exmouth Rd. *Ayl* —4C **12** (in two parts)
Exmouth Rd. *Bud S* —4B **24**
Exton La. *Ext* —6A **18**
Exton Rd. *Mar B* —3A **10**
Exview Cotts. *Exmin* —4A **16**
Exwick Ct. *Exe* —4F **3**
Exwick La. *Exe* —5D **2** (in two parts)
Exwick Rd. *Exe* —4F **3**
Exwick Vs. *Exe* —5F **3**

Fairfax Gdns. *Exe* —4H **9**
Fairfield Av. *Exe* —4G **5**
Fairfield Clo. *Exm* —3D **22**
Fairfield Rd. *Exe* —6H **9**
Fairfield Rd. *Exm* —3D **22**
Fairfield Ter. *Exe* —2G **9** (6A **26**)
Fairhazel Dri. *Exe* —5F **3**
Fairlynch Museum & Arts Centre. —5F **25**
Fairmead Ct. *Exe* —3A **6**
Fairpark Clo. *Exe* —1B **10**
Fairpark Rd. *Exe* —1A **10** (4D **26**)
Fairview Av. *Cly M* —4F **13**
Fairview Ter. *Exe* —3B **6**
Fairview Ter. *Exm* —2D **22**
Fairway, The. *Exe* —3C **4**
Falcon Rd. *Sow I* —2A **12**
Falkland Clo. *Exe* —2C **4**
Fancett Clo. *Exe* —4A **6**
Farleys Ct. *Top* —3E **17**
Farm Clo. *Exe* —2G **11**
Farm Hill. *Exe* —4D **2**
Farmhouse Av. *Exe* —4B **6**
Farmhouse Ri. *Exmin* —4H **15**
Featherbed La. *Exm* —5C **20**
Featherstone Rd. *Exm* —5C **20**
Feltrim Av. *Exe* —3B **10**
Ferndale Gdns. *Exe* —2G **9**
Ferndale Rd. *Exe* —2G **9**
Fernpark Clo. *Exe* —4C **10**
Ferry Rd. *Top* —3E **17**
Festive Way. *Exmin* —4A **16**
Filmer Way. *Mar B* —3H **9**
Fingle Clo. *Exe* —4E **3**
Firs Pk. *Bak H* —3C **8**
First Av. *Exe* —6D **4** (EX1)
First Av. *Exe* —1C **16** (EX2)
Flayes Almshouses. *Exe* —4G **5**
Florida Dri. *Exe* —2A **4**
Flowerpot La. *Exe* —1G **9**
Flower St. *Wood* —5G **19**
Follett Rd. *Top* —3E **17**
Fordland Bottom Rd. *Long* —4A **8** (in two parts)
Fords Rd. *Exe* —2H **9** (6B **26**)
Fore Hill. *Bud S* —4F **25**
Fore St. *Bud S* —5E **25**
Fore St. *Exe* —1H **9** (3A **26**)
Fore St. *Exm* —3C **22**
Fore St. *Hea* —1D **10**
Fore St. *Ide* —4E **9**
Fore St. *Top* —3F **17**
Fore St. Cen. *Exe* —3A **26**
Forge Clo. *Bud S* —3D **24**
Fortescue Rd. *Exe* —3H **9**
Forton Rd. *Exm* —6E **21**
Fountain Hill. *Bud S* —5D **24**
Fouracre Clo. *Exe* —3E **5**
Fowey Clo. *Exe* —5D **4**
Fowler Clo. *Exmin* —4A **16**
Foxhayes Rd. *Exe* —6F **3**
Foxholes Hill. *Exm* —5E **23**
Fox Rd. *Exe* —2F **5**
Foxtor Rd. *Exe* —4E **3**
Frances Homes. *Exe* —6B **4**
Francis Clo. *Exe* —2F **9**
Francis Ct. *Exe* —1C **10**
Franklin St. *Exe* —1A **10** (4D **26**)
Franklyn Clo. *Exe* —3F **9**
Franklyn Dri. *Exe* —3F **9**
Fraser Rd. *Exm* —5F **21**
Freelands Clo. *Exm* —1F **23**
Frewins. *Bud S* —3D **24**
Friars Ga. *Exe* —1A **10** (4C **26**)
Friars' Wlk. *Exe* —1A **10** (4C **26**)
Friernhay St. *Exe* —1H **9** (3A **26**)
Frobisher Rd. *Exm* —5E **21**
Frog La. *Cly M* —3C **12**
Frog St. *Exe* —1H **9** (4A **26**)

Fulford Rd. *Exe* —5D **4**
Fulford Way. *Wood* —5G **19**
Fullers Ct. *Exe* —1H **9** (4B **26**)
Furze Rd. *Wood* —5G **19**

Gables, The. *Exm* —3F **23**
Gabriel Ct. *Exe* —4B **26**
Gallahad Clo. *Exe* —3E **5**
Galmpton Ri. *Exe* —3C **4**
Galsworthy Sq. *Exe* —4G **5**
Gandy St. *Exe* —6H **3** (1B **26**)
Garden Clo. *Exe* —2G **11**
Garden Ct. *Bud S* —4E **25**
Gareth Cres. *Exe* —2D **4**
Garland Clo. *Exe* —4D **2**
Garratt Clo. *Exm* —4E **21**
Garside Rd. *Exe* —6A **10**
Gater La. *Exe* —1A **10** (3C **26**)
Geneva Clo. *Exe* —2C **10**
Georges Clo. *Exe* —6F **5**
George St. *Exe* —1H **9** (3B **26**)
George St. *Exm* —2C **22**
Gervase Av. *Exe* —2H **9** (5A **26**)
Gibraltar Rd. *Lymp* —1A **20**
Gibson Clo. *Exm* —6G **21**
Gilbert Av. *Exe* —2G **11**
Gipsy Hill La. *Exe* —4B **6**
Gipsy La. *Exe* —4B **6**
Gipsy La. *Exm* —1C **22**
Gissons. *Exmin* —4B **16**
Gittisham Clo. *Exe* —6H **5**
Glade Way. *Cly M* —4G **13**
Gladstone Rd. *Exe* —6C **4**
Glasshouse La. *Exe* —6E **11**
Glastonbury Clo. *Exe* —2E **5**
Glave Saunders Av. *Exe* —2G **11**
Glebe Clo. *Exm* —2H **23**
Glebe Clo. *Lymp* —1A **20**
Glebelands. *Exmin* —4A **16**
Glebelands. *Lymp* —1A **20**
Glen Clo. *Cly M* —4G **13**
Glenmore Rd. *Exe* —1E **11**
Glenorchy Ct. Exm —2C 22 (off Exeter Rd.)
Glenthorne Rd. *Exe* —3G **3**
Glen Wlk. *Exe* —2B **4**
Glenwood Ri. *Exe* —2B **10**
Globefield. *Top* —3F **17**
Globe Hill. *Wood* —5F **19**
Globe La. *Top* —4F **17**
Gloucester Rd. *Exe* —5E **3**
Gloucester Rd. *Exm* —4F **21**
Goat Wlk. *Top* —5F **17**
Goldsmith St. *Exe* —6H **3** (2B **26**)
Goldsmith St. *Hea* —6D **4**
Good Shepherd Dri. *Exe* —1A **10** (4D **26**)
Gordon Rd. *Exe* —5C **4**
Gordon Rd. *Top* —2E **17**
Gore La. *Exm* —4G **23**
Gorfin Clo. *Exm* —1G **23**
Gorse La. *Exm* —3F **21**
Goverts. *Wood* —5G **19**
Goy Gth. *Exe* —3B **4**
Grace Rd. *Mar B* —4H **9**
Grafton Rd. *Exe* —3G **3** (in three parts)
Grainger Clo. *Exe* —1G **11**
Granary La. *Bud S* —3F **25**
Grandisson Ct. *Exe* —4E **11**
Grange Av. *Exm* —1D **22**
Grange Clo. *Exm* —1D **22**
Grange Clo. *Lymp* —2B **20**
Grasslands Dri. *Exe* —4B **6**
Gt. Duryard Cotts. *Exe* —2F **3**
Great Exmouth OO Model Railway, The. —4C **22**
Gt. Hill Vw. *Exe* —2C **4**
Greatwood Ter. *Top* —3E **17**
Grecian Way. *Exe* —2G **11**
Greenacres. *Exe* —1G **3**
Green Clo. *Exm* —1E **23**
Greendale La. *Cly M* —6H **13**
Greenhaven. *Bud S* —3D **24**
Greenhill Av. *Exm* —2E **23**
Greenhill Av. *Lymp* —2A **20**
Green La. *Exe* —1E **9**
Green La. *Ext* —6H **17**
Green M. *Bud S* —4E **25**
Greenpark Av. *Exe* —5H **5**
Greenpark Rd. *Exm* —5F **21**
Green, The. *Exm* —1H **23**
Green, The. *Ide* —5D **8**
Greenway. *Exe* —3E **9**
Greenway. *Wood* —5F **19**
Greenway La. *Bud S* —3D **24**
Greenwood Av. *Exe* —1H **11**
Grenadier Rd. *Exe B* —5A **6**
Grendon Bldgs. *Exe* —3B **26**
Grendon Rd. *Exe* —6C **4**
Grenville Av. *Exe* —4H **5**
Grenville Rd. *Exm* —5E **21**
Grindle Way. *Cly M* —4D **12**
Grove Hill. *Top* —3F **17**
Grovsvenor Pl. *Exe* —5B **4**
Guildford Clo. *Exe* —6E **3**
Guildhall Shop. Cen. *Exe* —2B **26**
Guinea St. *Exe* —1H **9** (3B **26**)
Guinevere Way. *Exe* —3E **5**
Guinness La. *Exe* —4E **3**
Gussiford La. *Exm* —3C **22**
Guys Rd. *Exe* —6F **3**

Haccombe Clo. *Exe* —1E **9**
Hadlow Vw. Ter. *Exe* —1D **10**
Hadrian Dri. *Exe* —6E **3**
Hadrians Way. *Exm* —6F **21**
Haldon Clo. *Top* —2E **17**
Haldon Ct. *Exm* —5D **20**
Haldon Rd. *Exe* —6G **3** (1A **26**)
Halscombe La. *Ide* —6A **8**
Halsdon Av. *Exm* —6C **20**
Halsdon La. *Exm* —6C **20**
Halsdon Rd. *Exm* —2C **22**
Halse Hill. *Bud S* —4D **24**
Halses Clo. *Exe* —4D **2**
Halsfordwood La. *Nadd* —4A **2**
Halyards. *Top* —3E **17**
Hambeer La. *Exe* —3E **9**
Hamilton Av. *Exe* —4D **10**
Hamilton Dri. *Exe* —1H **11**
Hamilton Rd. *Exm* —2F **23**
Hamilton Rd. *Top* —2E **17**
Hamlin Gdns. *Exe* —5E **5**
Hamlin La. *Exe* —5E **5**
Hamlyns La. *Exe* —3D **2**
Hammond Cft. Way. *Exe* —6H **9**
Hampden Pl. *Exe* —5A **26**
Hampshire Clo. *Exe* —2E **9**
Hampstead La. *Ext* —5H **17**
Hampton Bldgs. *Exe* —5B **4**
Hams, The. *Ide* —5D **8**
Hanover Clo. *Exe* —6D **4**
Hanover Ct. *Exe* —5A **10**
Hanover Rd. *Exe* —6D **4**
Harbour Ct. *Exm* —3A **22**
Hardy Rd. *Exe* —1H **11**
Harebell Copse. *Exe* —6H **3**
Harefield Clo. *Exe* —4G **3**
Harefield Dri. *Lymp* —2B **20**
Harefield Rd. *Lymp* —1B **20**
Harlequins Cen. *Exe* —1B **26**
Harper Wlk. *Exm* —3E **23**
Harrier Way. *Sow I* —2A **12**
Harringcourt Dri. *Exe* —2A **6**
Harringcourt Rd. *Exe* —2A **6**
Harrington Gdns. *Exe* —3A **6**
Harrington La. *Exe* —2G **5**
Harrison Ho. *Exe* —3H **5**
Hartley Rd. *Exm* —3C **22**
Hartopp Rd. *Exm* —2C **22**
Harts Clo. *Exe* —4A **6**
Harts La. *Exe* —4G **5**
Harwood Clo. *Exm* —6F **21**
Hatherleigh Rd. *Exe* —4G **9**
Haven Clo. *Exe* —2H **9** (6B **26**)
Haven Rd. *Exe* —2H **9** (5A **26**)
Havitree Rd. *Exe* —6B **4**
Hawthorne Gro. *Exm* —6G **21**
Hawthorn Rd. *Exe* —3D **10**
Hawthorn Way. *Alp* —6G **9**
Hayes Barton Ct. *Exe* —1G **9**
Hayes Clo. *Bud S* —3E **25**
Hayley Rd. *Exm* —5E **21**
Hayne Clo. *Exe* —5E **5**
Haynes La. *Long* —4A **8**
Haytor Dri. *Exe* —5E **3**
Hazeldene Gdns. *Exm* —6C **20**
Hazelmead Rd. *Cly M* —4F **13**
Hazel Rd. *Exe* —4D **10**
Headingley Clo. *Exe* —2G **11**
Headland Clo. *Exe* —5G **5**
Headland Cres. *Exe* —5G **5**
Headon Gdns. *Exe* —5E **11**
Heard Av. *Exm* —1G **23**
Hearts of Oaks. *Exe* —1A **12**
Heath Barton. *Pin* —3G **5**
Heather Clo. *Exe* —6F **5**
Heatherdale. *Exm* —3E **23**
Heath Rd. *Exe* —2F **11**
Heavitree Pk. *Exe* —1E **11**
Helena Pl. *Exm* —3C **22**
Hele Rd. *Exe* —5G **3**
Hellings Pk. La. *Broad* —1G **7**
Hendy Gdns. *Exe* —5F **3**
Henley Rd. *Exm* —2E **23**
Hennock Ct. *Exe* —5B **10**
Hennock Rd. *Mar B* —4A **10**
Henrietta Pl. Exm —2C 22 (off Henrietta Rd.)
Henrietta Rd. *Exm* —2C **22**
Hensleigh Dri. *Exe* —1C **10**
Herbert Rd. *Exe* —5D **4**
Hereford Clo. *Exm* —4F **21**
Hereford Rd. *Exe* —6D **2**
Heron Ct. *Exm* —3E **23**
Heron Ind. Units. *Exe* —1A **12**
Heron Rd. *Exe* —3D **8**
Heron Rd. *Sow I* —1A **12**
Herschell Rd. *Exe* —4C **4**
Hexworthy Av. *Exe* —4E **3**
Highbury Pk. *Exm* —6C **20**
Highcliffe Clo. *Lymp* —3A **20**
High Cft. *Exe* —3G **3**
Highcross Rd. *Exe* —5A **4**
Higher Aboveway. *Exmin* —5B **16**
Higher Barley Mt. *Exe* —6E **3**
Higher Bedlands. *Bud S* —3D **24**
Higher Hoopern La. *Exe* —3A **4**
Higher King's Av. *Exe* —3B **4**
Higher Marley Rd. *Exm* —3F **21**
Higher Rd. *Wood S* —1E **19**
Higher Shapter Clo. *Top* —4F **17**
Higher Shapter St. *Top* —4F **17**
Higher Summerlands. *Exe* —6B **4**
Higher Wear Rd. *Exe* —1C **16**
Highfield. *Top* —1F **17**
Highfield La. *Exm* —3D **22**
High Meadows. *Exe* —1E **9**
High St. Arc. *Exe* —6A **4** (1D **26**)
High St. Budleigh Salterton, *Bud S* —5E **25**
High St. Exeter, *Exe* —6H **3** (2B **26**)
High St. Exmouth, *Exm* —3C **22**
High St. Ide, *Ide* —5D **8**
High St. Topsham, *Top* —2E **17**
High Vw. Gdns. *Exm* —2D **22**
Hill Barton Bus. Pk. *Cly M* —3H **13**
Hill Barton La. *Exe* —5G **5** (in two parts)
Hill Barton Rd. *Exe* —4H **5**
Hill Clo. *Exe* —3B **4**
Hill Crest. *Exmin* —4A **16**
Hillcrest Pk. *Exe* —2A **4**
Hill Dri. *Exm* —4D **20**
Hill La. *Exe* —5F **5** (in three parts)
Hill Pk. Clo. *Exe* —5G **5**
Hill Ri. *Exe* —5G **5**
Hillsborough Av. *Exe* —5A **4**
Hillside Av. *Exe* —5A **4**
Hillyfield Rd. *Exe* —5G **5**
Hoker Rd. *Exe* —1E **11**
Holland Rd. *Exe* —2F **9**
Holland Rd. *Exm* —6F **21**
Holley Clo. *Exmin* —4A **16**
Holloway St. *Exe* —1A **10** (4C **26**)
Hollow La. *Exe* —5H **5**
Hollowpits Ct. *Exe* —6G **9**
Hollows, The. *Exm* —2D **22**
Hollymount Clo. *Exm* —4E **21**

Holly Rd. *Exe* —3D **10**
Holly Wlk. *Exm* —4F **21**
Holman Way. *Top* —4F **17**
Holne Ct. *Exe* —4E **3**
Holne Ri. *Exe* —2F **11**
Homefield Rd. *Exe* —6D **4**
Hometor Ct. *Exm* —1C **22**
Honeylands Dri. *Exe* —5E **5**
Honeylands Way. *Exe* —5E **5**
Honey La. *Exe* —2B **6**
Honey La. *Wood S* —1G **19**
Honey Pk. Rd. *Bud S* —3F **25**
Honeysuckle Ct. *Exe* —4D **2**
Honiton Rd. *Exe* —1F **11**
Hooker Clo. *Bud S* —3D **24**
Hoopern Av. *Exe* —3A **4**
Hoopern La. *Exe* —4A **4**
Hoopern St. *Exe* —5A **4**
Hope Pl. *Exe* —1E **11**
Hope Rd. *Exe* —1E **11**
Hospital La. *Exe* —4G **5**
Howard Clo. *Exe* —4E **3**
Howell Rd. *Exe* —5G **3**
Hulham Rd. *Exm* —3E **21**
Hummingbird Clo. *Exe* —3A **6**
Hungry Fox Ind. Est. *Broad* —1G **7**
Hunton Clo. *Lymp* —2A **20**
Hurst Av. *Exe* —2F **11**
Hutchings Mead. *Exe* —4B **6**

Iddesleigh Rd. *Exe* —4C **4**
Ide La. *Exe* —3D **8**
(in two parts)
Idestone La. *Exe* —6C **8**
Ilex Clo. *Exe* —2F **5**
Ilex Clo. *Shi S* —4A **14**
Imperial Rd. *Exm* —2B **22**
Imperial St. *Exe* —1F **9**
Ingleside Ct. *Bud S* —4E **25**
Inner Ting Tong. *Bud S* —2A **24**
Iolanthe Dri. *Exe* —2E **5**
Iona Av. *Exm* —5C **20**
Iris Av. *Exe* —2H **9** (5A **26**)
Iron Bri. *Exe* —6H **3** (1A **26**)
Isca Rd. *Exe* —2H **9** (6B **26**)
Isca Rd. *Exm* —4E **23**
Isleworth Rd. *Exe* —1E **9**
Iveagh Ct. *Exe* —4F **3**
Ivy Clo. *Exe* —2E **11**
Ivydale. *Exm* —4F **21**

James Ct. *Exe* —1A **10** (3C **26**)
Jarvis Clo. *Exm* —2G **23**
(in two parts)
Jennifer Clo. *Exe* —3C **10**
Jesmond Rd. *Exe* —5C **4**
Jocelyn Rd. *Bud S* —3E **25**
John Hudson Way. *Exm* —2G **23**
John Levers Way. *Exe* —1F **9**
John St. *Exe* —1H **9** (3B **26**)
Jubilee Clo. *Exmin* —4B **16**
Jubilee Dri. *Exm* —4E **21**
Jubilee Gro. *Lymp* —2B **20**
Jubilee Rd. *Exe* —5C **4**
Jubilee Sq. *Top* —4F **17**
Juniper Clo. *Exe* —2F **5**
Jupes Clo. *Exmin* —5B **16**

Kalenderhay La. *Exe* —6H **3** (3B **26**)
Kay Clo. *Exm* —1E **23**
Keats Clo. *Exm* —3E **21**
Kenbury Dri. *Exe* —6A **10**
Kendall Clo. *Exe* —5B **4**
Kennerley Av. *Exe* —4F **5**
Kennford Rd. *Mar B* —3H **9**
Kenn La. *Exmin* —6H **15**
Kent Clo. *Exe* —2E **11**
Kersbrook La. *Kers* —2E **25**
Kerswill Rd. *Exe* —2F **9**
Kestor Dri. *Exe* —4E **3**
Kestrel Way. *Sow I* —1A **12**
Keverel Rd. *Exm* —6C **20**
Kilbarran Ri. *Exe* —4G **3**
Kimberley Rd. *Exe* —1A **10** (4D **26**)
King Arthur's Rd. *Exe* —2D **4**
King Edward St. *Exe* —3G **3**
Kingfisher Av. *Exe* —2D **8**
Kingfisher Dri. *Exe* —2B **4**
Kingfisher Way. *Sow I* —1A **12**
King Henrys Rd. *Exe* —3C **10**
Kingsgate. *Exe* —4A **4**
Kingslake Ct. *Exm* —1C **22**
Kingsley Av. *Exe* —4F **5**
King's Rd. *Exe* —4C **4**
King Stephen Clo. *Exe* —5A **4**
Kingston Rd. *Exm* —2E **23**
King St. *Exe* —1H **9** (3B **26**)
King St. *Exm* —3C **22**
Kingsway. *Exe* —1D **10**
King's Wharf. *Exe* —4C **26**
Kingswood Clo. *Exe* —4E **3**
King William St. *Exe* —6A **4** (1D **26**)
Kinnerton Ct. *Exe* —4F **3**
Kinnerton Way. *Exe* —4E **3**
Kipling Dri. *Exe* —2D **10**
Knightley Rd. *Exe* —3C **10**
Knights Cres. *Exe* —3H **11**
Knowle Dri. *Exe* —5E **3**
Knowle Hill. *Bud S* —3A **24**
Knowle M. *Bud S* —2B **24**
Knowle Rd. *Bud S* —3C **24**
Knowle Village. *Bud S* —4B **24**

Laburnham Clo. *Exm* —4F **21**
Laburnum Rd. *Exe* —3D **10**
Lackaborough Ct. *Exe* —6G **9**
Ladysmith Rd. *Exe* —5D **4**
Lakelands Dri. *Exe* —6F **3**
Lakeside Av. *Exe* —6F **11**
Lamacraft Dri. *Exe* —5E **5**
Lamb All. *Exe* —2C **26**
Lamplough Rd. *Exm* —4C **20**
Lancaster Clo. *Exe* —1F **11**
Lancelot Rd. *Exe* —2E **5**
Landhays Rd. *Exe* —1F **9**
Landscore Rd. *Exe* —1F **9**
Lands Rd. *Exe* —3H **5**
Langaton Gdns. *Exe* —3B **6**
Langaton La. *Exe* —3B **6**
Langerwehe Way. *Exm* —3B **22**
Langstone Dri. *Exm* —5E **21**
Lansdowne. *Exe* —2F **11**
Lansdowne Rd. *Bud S* —4B **24**
Lansdowne Ter. *Exe* —1A **10** (4D **26**)
Larch Clo. *Exm* —4F **21**
Larch Rd. *Exe* —3F **9**
Larkbeare Rd. *Exe* —2A **10** (5D **26**)
Larson Yd. *Bud S* —3F **25**
Latimer Rd. *Exe* —4E **5**
Laurel Ri. *Exm* —1F **23**
Laurel Rd. *Exe* —3D **10**
Lawn Rd. *Exm* —2C **22**
Lawn, The. *Bud S* —5E **25**
Lawrence Av. *Exe* —2G **9**
Laxton Av. *Exe* —6G **5**
Leas Rd. *Bud S* —4E **25**
Lebanon Clo. *Exe* —3C **4**
Legion Way. *Exe* —5H **9**
Leighdene Clo. *Exe* —2C **10**
Leighton Ter. *Exe* —5A **4**
Leslie Rd. *Exm* —1C **22**
Lestock Clo. *Exm* —2G **23**
Lethbridge Rd. *Exe* —1F **11**
Lewis Cres. *Exe* —3H **11**
Leypark Clo. *Exe* —5G **5**
Leypark Cres. *Exe* —6G **5**
Leypark Rd. *Exe* —5G **5**
Lichgate Rd. *Exe* —6H **9**
Liffey Ri. *Exe* —4E **3**
Lilac Rd. *Exe* —3D **10**
Lily Mt. *Exe* —4D **2**
Lime Gro. *Exmin* —4A **16**
Lime Gro. *Exm* —4E **21**
Limegrove Rd. *Exe* —1F **9**
Lime Kiln La. *Exe* —5E **11**
Limekiln La. *Exm* —4E **23**
Lime Tree Clo. *Exe* —3G **11**
Lincoln Clo. *Exm* —3G **21**
Lincoln Rd. *Exe* —6E **3**
Linda Clo. *Exe* —1F **11**
Linden Clo. *Exm* —5F **21**
Linden Va. *Exe* —5H **3**
Linfield Gdns. *Exe* —2F **9**
Links Clo. *Exm* —2E **23**
Links Rd. *Bud S* —5C **24**
Linnet Clo. *Exe* —2B **4**
Lisa Clo. *Exe* —2E **11**
Litchfield Rd. *Exe* —6D **2**
Lit. Bicton Pl. *Exm* —3C **22**
Lit. Castle St. *Exe* —6A **4** (1C **26**)
Littledown Clo. *Exm* —2H **23**
Lit. Down La. *Bud S* —1E **25**
Littleham Chu. Path. *Exm* —5A **24**
Littleham Rd. *Exm* —2F **23**
Littleham Village. *Lit* —2H **23**
Lit. John's Cross Hill. *Exe* —3E **9**
Lit. Knowle. *Bud S* —4D **24**
Lit. Knowle Ct. *Bud S* —4D **24**
Littlemead La. *Exm* —4C **20**
Lit. Meadow. *Exm* —4F **21**
Lit. Queen St. *Exe* —6A **4** (2C **26**)
Lit. Rack St. *Exe* —1H **9** (3B **26**)
Lit. Silver. *Exe* —5H **3** (1A **26**)
Lit. Silver La. *Matf* —3F **15**
Little Way. *Exe* —3F **9**
Liverton Bus. Pk. *Exm* —6H **21**
Liverton Clo. *Exm* —1G **23**
Liverton Copse Nature Reserve. —6H **21**
Livery Dole Almshouses. *Exe* —1C **10**
Lloyds Ct. *Exe* —4G **5**
Lloyds Cres. *Exe* —5G **5**
Locarno Rd. *Exe* —2F **9**
Lockfield Ct. *Alp* —5H **9**
Locksley Clo. *Exe* —6E **11**
Lodge Hill. *Exe* —4G **3**
Longacres. *Exe* —1B **10**
Longbrook La. *Lymp* —3A **20**
Longbrook St. *Exe* —5A **4** (1D **26**)
Longbrook Ter. *Exe* —5A **4**
Long Causeway. *Exm* —3D **22**
Long Copp. *Bud S* —3E **25**
Longdown Rd. *Long* —4A **8**
Long La. *Exm* —3E **23**
(in two parts)
Longmeadow. *Cly M* —3C **12**
Longmeadow. *Wood* —5G **19**
Longmeadow Rd. *Lymp* —2B **20**
Long Pk. *Wood* —5G **19**
Lonsdale Rd. *Exe* —1E **11**
Looe Rd. *Exe* —5G **3**
Loram Way. *Exe* —6A **10**
Lords Way. *Exe* —3G **11**
Louisa Pl. *Exm* —3C **22**
Louisa Ter. *Exm* —4C **22**
Lovelace Cres. *Exm* —1E **23**
Lovelace Gdns. *Exe* —6H **9**
Lovell Clo. *Exm* —4E **21**
Lwr. Albert St. *Exe* —6B **4**
Lwr. Argyll Rd. *Exe* —3G **3**
Lower Av. *Exe* —6D **4**
Lwr. Coombe St. *Exe* —1H **9** (4B **26**)
Lwr. Fore St. *Exm* —3C **22**
Lwr. Harrington La. *Exe* —3A **6**
Lwr. Hill Barton Rd. *Exe* —6G **5**
Lwr. King's Av. *Exe* —4B **4**
Lwr. North St. *Exe* —6H **3** (1A **26**)
Lower Rd. *Wood S* —1E **19**
Lwr. St German's St. *Exe* —4A **4**
Lwr. Shapter St. *Top* —4F **17**
Lwr. Shillingford. *Shi A* —2C **14**
Lwr. Summerlands. *Exe* —6B **4**
Lwr. Wear Rd. *Exe* —6E **11**
Lucas Av. *Exe* —4B **4**
Lucky La. *Exe* —1A **10** (4C **26**)
Ludwell La. *Exe* —2E **11**
Lustleigh Clo. *Mar B* —5A **10**
Lymebourne Av. *Exe* —6E **5**
Lyncombe Clo. *Exe* —3C **4**

Lyndhurst Rd. *Exe* —1C **10**
Lyndhurst Rd. *Exm* —1C **22**
Lynwood Av. *Exe* —1G **9**

Madagascan Clo. *Exm* —1G **23**
Maddocks Row. *Exe* —6H **3** (1B **26**)
Madeira Ct. *Exm* —4D **22**
Madeira Vs. *Exm* —2C **22**
Madeira Wlk. *Bud S* —5F **25**
Madison Av. *Exe* —6E **5**
Maer Bay Ct. *Exm* —4D **22**
Maer La. *Lit* —4E **23**
Maer Rd. *Exm* —4E **23**
Maer Va. *Exm* —3E **23**
Magdalen Cotts. *Exe* —1B **10**
Magdalen Gdns. *Exe* —1C **10**
Magdalen Rd. *Exe* —1B **10**
Magdalen St. *Exe* —1A **10** (3C **26**)
Magnolia Av. *Exe* —3E **11**
Magnolia Av. *Exm* —1G **23**
*Magnolia Cen. Exm —3C **22***
(off Chapel St.)
Magnolia Wlk. *Exm* —3C **22**
Magpie Cres. *Exo P* —2D **8**
Main Rd. *Exmin* —2A **16**
(in two parts)
Main Rd. *Pin* —3A **6**
Majorfield Rd. *Top* —3F **17**
Mallard Rd. *Sow I* —1A **12**
Mallison Clo. *Exe* —4F **3**
Malvern Gdns. *Exe* —2E **11**
Mamhead Rd. *Exe* —2G **11**
Mamhead Vw. *Exm* —3A **22**
Manaton Clo. *Mar B* —5A **10**
Manaton Ct. *Exe* —6A **10**
Manchester Rd. *Exm* —3B **22**
Manchester St. *Exm* —2B **22**
Mandrake Clo. *Exe* —5H **9**
Mandrake Rd. *Exe* —5G **9**
Manor Pk. *Cly M* —3C **12**
Manor Rd. *Exe* —1G **9**
Mansfield Rd. *Exe* —4C **4**
Masefield Rd. *Exe* —4G **5**
Mansfield Ter. *Bud S* —3F **25**
Manson Gro. *Exm* —6C **20**
Manston Rd. *Exe* —5C **4**
Manston Ter. *Exe* —1C **10**
Manstree Rd. *Shi S* —4A **14**
Manstree Ter. *Shi S* —4A **14**
Maple Dri. *Exm* —4F **21**
Maple Rd. *Exe* —1F **9**
Marcom Clo. *Exm* —4F **21**
Marcus Rd. *Exm* —6F **21**
Margaret Rd. *Exe* —3C **4**
*Margaret St. Exm —3C **22***
(off Chapel St.)
Marina Ct. *Exm* —4D **22**
Marine Ct. *Bud S* —5F **25**
Marine Pde. *Bud S* —5F **25**
Marine Way. *Exm* —2C **22**
Marions Way. *Exm* —5F **21**
Maristow Av. *Exm* —5D **20**
Market St. *Exe* —1H **9** (3B **26**)
Market St. *Exm* —3C **22**
Markham La. *Exe* —1A **14**
(in two parts)
Marlborough Clo. *Exm* —5G **21**
Marlborough Ct. *Exe* —6A **10**
Marlborough Dri. *Exe* —1H **11**
Marlborough Rd. *Exe* —1B **10**
Marles, The. *Exm* —5E **21**
Marley Dri. *Lymp* —2F **21**
Marley Rd. *Exm* —5D **20**
(in two parts)
Marpool Cres. *Exm* —1E **23**
Marpool Hill. *Exm* —2D **22**
Marsh Barton Rd. *Mar B* —3H **9**
Marsh Barton Trad. Est. *Mar B* —4A **10**
Marsh Grn. Rd. *Mar B* —3A **10**
Marsh La. *Cly G* —2G **17**
(in two parts)
Marshrow La. *Exmin* —6B **16**
Martins Clo. *Exm* —5G **21**
Martins La. *Exe* —6A **4** (2C **26**)
Mary Arches St. *Exe* —6H **3** (2A **26**)
Maryfield Av. *Exe* —4B **4**
Masey Rd. *Exm* —1F **23**
Matfield. *Lymp* —2B **20**
Matford Av. *Exe* —2B **10**
Matford Bus. Pk. *Exe* —6B **10**
Matford La. *Exe* —2B **10**
Matford M. *Alp* —1G **15**
Matford Pk. Rd. *Mar B* —5A **10**
Matford Rd. *Exe* —2B **10**
Matthews Ct. *Exe* —2H **5**
Mayfield Dri. *Exm* —3F **23**
Mayfield Rd. *Pin* —3A **6**
Mayfield Rd. *St L* —1E **11**
Mayflower Av. *Exe* —2B **4**
Maypole Rd. *Exe* —3D **4**
Maypole Wlk. *Exe* —3D **4**
May St. *Exe* —5B **4**
Mead Cotts. *Exm* —2H **23**
Meadowbrook Clo. *Exe* —4E **3**
Meadow Clo. *Bud S* —4D **24**
Meadow Clo. *Cly M* —3G **13**
Meadow Clo. *Lymp* —2B **20**
Meadow La. *Bud S* —4E **25**
Meadow Path. *Exe* —6D **4**
Meadow Rd. *Bud S* —5D **24**
Meadow St. *Exm* —2C **22**
Meadow Vw. Rd. *Exm* —5G **21**
Meadow Way. *Exe* —1D **10**
Mede, The. *Exe* —4F **5**
Mede, The. *Top* —3E **17**
Meeting La. *Lymp* —1A **20**
Meeting St. *Exm* —2C **22**
Meetways La. *Exm* —3F **23**
Melbourne Pl. *Exe* —1A **10** (5D **26**)
Melbourne St. *Exe* —2A **10**
Meldon Ct. *Bud S* —4F **25**
Membury Clo. *Exe* —6H **5**
Mercer Ct. *Exe* —4E **11**
Meresyke. *Exm* —3E **23**
Merlin Cres. *Exe* —3E **5**
Mermaid Ct. *Exe* —3B **26**
Merrion Av. *Exm* —3F **23**
Merrivale Rd. *Exe* —2F **9**
Michigan Way. *Exe* —2A **4**
Middle Moor. *Exe* —1H **11**
Midway. *Exm* —1G **23**
Midway Clo. *Exe* —5G **9**
Midway Ter. *Exe* —5G **9**
Milbury Clo. *Exmin* —3B **16**
Milbury La. *Exmin* —4B **16**
Mildmay Clo. *Exe* —5F **3**
Mile Gdns. *Exe* —2D **4**
Mile La. *Exe* —1D **4**
(in two parts)
Millbrook La. *Exe* —4D **10**
Mill Dri. *Exe* —5D **10**
Miller Clo. *Exe* —2G **11**
Miller Way. *Exmin* —3H **15**
Milletts Clo. *Exmin* —4A **16**
Mill La. *Cly H* —4E **7**
Mill La. *Exe* —5H **9**
(nr. Church Rd.)
Mill La. *Exe* —5D **10**
(nr. Mill Rd., in two parts)
Mill La. *Ext* —6A **18**
Mill Rd. *Exe* —5D **10**
Mill Yd. *Exe* —5D **10**
Milton La. *Exm* —2E **23**
Milton Rd. *Exe* —3D **10**
Mincinglake Rd. *Sto H* —3C **4**
Minster Rd. *Exmin* —3B **16**
Mint, The. *Exe* —1H **9** (3A **26**)
Mirey La. *Wood* —5F **19**
Mission Ct. *Exe* —4A **26**
Mitre La. *Exe* —6H **3** (2B **26**)
Modred Clo. *Exe* —3E **5**
Monkerton Dri. *Exe* —4A **6**
Monks Rd. *Exe* —5C **4**
Monkswell Rd. *Exe* —4C **4**
Monmouth Av. *Top* —4F **17**
Monmouth Hill. *Top* —4F **17**
Monmouth St. *Top* —4F **17**
Montague Gdns. *Bud S* —4C **24**
Montery Gdns. *Exe* —3C **4**
Mont-Le-Grand. *Exe* —6C **4**
Montpellier Rd. *Exm* —3C **22**
Mony-Le-Grand Rd. *Exe* —6D **4**
Moonhill Clo. *Exe* —6A **10**
Moonridge. *Exe* —1C **16**
Moorfield Clo. *Exm* —1E **23**
Moorfield Rd. *Exm* —1D **22**
Moor Haven. *Bud S* —3D **24**
Moorlands Rd. *Bud S* —4B **24**
Moorland Way. *Exe* —4E **3**
Moor La. *Bud S* —3D **24**
Moor La. *Cly M* —3C **18**
Moor La. *Sow I* —6A **6**
Moormead. *Bud S* —4D **24**
Moorpark. *Exm* —3E **23**
Moorview Clo. *Exe* —3B **4**
Moreton Cres. *Exm* —3B **22**
Morley Rd. *Exe* —4C **4**
Morton Cres. M. *Exm* —3B **22**
Morton Rd. *Exm* —3B **22**
Morven Dri. *Exm* —5C **20**
Mosshayne La. *Exe* —1C **6**
(in two parts)
Mountain Clo. *Exm* —1H **23**
Mt. Batten Clo. *Exm* —5F **21**
Mt. Dinham. *Exe* —2A **26**
Mt. Howe. *Exe* —4G **17**
Mt. Pleasant Av. *Exm* —4D **20**
Mt. Pleasant Ct. *Exm* —5D **20**
Mt. Pleasant Rd. *Exe* —4C **4**
Mt. Radford Cres. *Exe* —1B **10**
*Mt. Radford Sq. Exe —1B **10***
(off Radford Rd.)
Mt. Wear Sq. *Exe* —6F **11**
Mowbray Av. *Exe* —5A **4**
Mudbank La. *Exm* —6B **20**
Mulberry Clo. *Exe* —6F **5**
Musgrave Row. *Exe* —6A **4** (1C **26**)
Mutton La. *Exe* —6A **10**
Myrtle Clo. *Exe* —5H **9**
Myrtle Rd. *Exe* —2E **9**
Myrtle Row. *Exm* —3C **22**

Nadder Bottom. *White* —3A **2**
Nadder La. *White* —4B **2**
Nadder Pk. Rd. *Exe* —1D **8**
Napier Ter. *Exe* —6H **3** (2A **26**)
Nasmith Clo. *Exm* —6F **21**
Nelson Clo. *Top* —3E **17**
Nelson Dri. *Exm* —1G **23**
Nelson Rd. *Exe* —2G **9**
Nelson Way. *Exe* —1G **11**
New Bri. St. *Exe* —1H **9**
Newcombe St. *Exe* —6D **4**
Newcombe St. Gdns. *Exe* —6E **5**
*Newcombe Ter. Exe —6D **4***
(off S. Lawn Ter.)
Newcourt Rd. *Top* —6A **12**
Newfoundland Clo. *Exe* —2C **4**
Newham Ct. *Exe* —1E **9**
Newhayes Clo. *Exe* —4G **9**
Newlands Av. *Exm* —1F **23**
Newlands Clo. *Exe* —4G **9**
Newman Rd. *Exe* —2E **9**
New N. Rd. *Exe* —4G **3** (1C **26**)
New N. Rd. *Exm* —2C **22**
Newport Pk. *Exe* —1C **16**
Newport Rd. *Exe* —1C **16**
New St. *Exm* —2C **22**
*Newton Clo. Exe —6B **4***
(off Clifton St.)
New Valley. *Exe* —5F **3**
New Way. *Wood S* —2G **19**
New Way Bldgs. *Exm* —2C **22**
Nicholas Rd. *Exe* —6E **5**
Nightingale Wlk. *Exo P* —3D **8**
*Nineteen Steps. Bud S —5F **25***
(off Marine Pde.)
Norman Clo. *Exm* —5F **21**
Normandy Clo. *Exm* —6G **21**
Normandy Rd. *Exe* —6D **4**
Norman Stevens Clo. *Exm* —3E **23**
North Av. *Exe* —6C **4**
N. Bridge Pl. *Exe* —6H **3** (1A **26**)
Northernhay Ga. *Exe* —6H **3** (1B **26**)
Northernhay Pl. *Exe* —6A **4** (1C **26**)
Northernhay Sq. *Exe* —6H **3** (1B **26**)
Northernhay St. *Exe* —6H **3** (2B **26**)
N. Grange. *Exe* —3H **11**
N. Lawn Ct. *Exe* —6D **4**
N. Park Rd. *Exe* —3H **3**
North St. *Exe* —6H **3** (2B **26**)

North St. *Exm* —2C **22**
North St. *Hea* —6D **4**
North St. *Top* —4F **17**
Northview Rd. *Bud S* —5D **24**
Norwich Clo. *Exm* —3F **21**
Norwich Rd. *Exe* —6E **3**
Norwood Av. *Exe* —2B **10**
Nurseries Clo. *Top* —2E **17**
Nursery Clo. *Exm* —1E **23**
Nursery M. *Exm* —1E **23**
Nutbrook. *Exm* —6D **20**
Nutwell Rd. *Lymp* —1A **20**

Oak Clo. *Exmin* —4A **16**
Oak Clo. *Pin* —3A **6**
Oak Clo. *Shi A* —2C **14**
Oakfield Rd. *Exe* —1G **9**
Oakfield St. *Exe* —1D **10**
Oakhayes Rd. *Wood* —5F **19**
Oakleigh Rd. *Exm* —2D **22**
Oakley Clo. *Exe* —3A **6**
Oak Ridge. *Alp* —6G **9**
Oak Rd. *Exe* —2F **9**
Oaktree Clo. *Exm* —4D **20**
Oaktree Pl. *Mar B* —5A **10**
Oakwood Ri. *Exm* —4G **21**
Oberon Rd. *Exe B* —5A **6**
Oilmill La. *Cly M* —4E **13**
Okehampton Pl. *Exe* —1G **9** (4A **26**)
Okehampton Rd. *Exe* —1F **9**
Okehampton St. *Exe* —1G **9** (4A **26**)
Okewood Ct. *Exm* —4D **22**
Old Abbey Ct. *Exe* —3C **10**
Old Bakery Clo. *Exe* —5F **3**
Old Bystock Dri. *Exm* —3G **21**
Old Dawlish Rd. *Kennf* —6D **14**
Old Ebford La. *Ebf* —4A **18**
Oldfields. *Exm* —3E **23**
Old Ide La. *Ide* —4E **9**
Old Mkt. Clo. *Exe* —3H **9**
Old Matford La. *Matf* —1F **15**
Old Mill Clo. *Exe* —2B **10**
Old Okehampton Rd. *Exe* —5A **2**
Old Pk. Rd. *Exe* —5A **4**
Old Pavilion Clo. *Exe* —2G **11**
Old Pinn La. *Exe* —4A **6**
Old Rydon Clo. *Exe* —4A **12**
Old Ryton La. *Exe* —5G **11**
Old Sludge Beds Nature Reserve. —2C **16**
Old's Vw. *Exe* —5G **3**
Old Tiverton Rd. *Exe* —5B **4**
Old Vicarage Clo. *Exe* —5D **8**
Old Vicarage Rd. *Exe* —2G **9**
Orchard Clo. *Exe* —3B **6**
Orchard Clo. *Exm* —6D **20**
Orchard Clo. *Lymp* —2A **20**
Orchard Clo. *Wood* —5G **19**
Orchard Gdns. *Exe* —2F **9**
Orchard Hill. *Exe* —3E **9**
Orchard Vw. *Hea* —1D **10**
Orchard Way. *Top* —3E **17**
Orcombe Ct. *Exm* —1F **23**
Osprey Rd. *Sow I* —6B **6**
Otago Cotts. *Exe* —3C **10**
*Otterbourne Ct. Bud S —5F **25***
(off Coastguard Rd.)
Otter Ct. *Bud S* —4G **25**
Otter Ct. *Exe* —5A **10**
Ottervale Rd. *Bud S* —4G **25**
Outer Ting Tong. *Exm* —2A **24**
Oval Grn. *Exe* —2G **11**
Oxford Clo. *Exm* —3G **21**
Oxford Rd. *Exe* —5B **4**
Oxford St. *Exe* —2G **9**

P**alace Cotts. Exm —2C **22
(off Parade)
Palace Ga. *Exe* —1A **10** (3C **26**)
Palm Clo. *Exm* —4F **21**
Palmer Ct. *Bud S* —4E **25**
Palmerston Dri. *Exe* —5E **3**
Pankhurst Clo. *Exm* —2G **23**
Panney, The. *Exe* —5E **5**
Parade. *Exm* —2C **22**
Paris St. *Exe* —6A **4** (1D **26**)
Paris St. Arc. *Exe* —6A **4** (1D **26**)
Park Clo. *Wood* —6G **19**
Parkers Cross La. *Exe* —2B **6**
Parkfield Rd. *Top* —3F **17**
Parkfield Way. *Top* —3F **17**
Parkhayes. *Wood S* —1G **19**
Parkhouse Rd. *Exe* —3F **9**
Parkland Dri. *Exe* —3G **11**
Park La. *Bud S* —4D **24**
Park La. *Exe* —1H **5**
Park La. *Exm* —1C **22**
Park Pl. *Hea* —6D **4**
Park Pl. *St Leo* —1B **10**
Park Rd. *Exe* —5C **4**
Park Rd. *Exm* —1C **22**
Parkside Cres. *Exe* —1B **6**
Parkside Dri. *Exm* —5F **21**
Parkside Rd. *Exe* —1B **6**
Parks La. *Bud S* —5F **25**
Parkway. *Exe* —3F **9**
Park Way. *Exm* —1E **23**
(in two parts)
Park Way. *Wood* —6G **19**
Parliament St. *Exe* —6H **3** (2B **26**)
Parr Clo. *Exe* —5B **4**
Parrish Way. *Exe* —5G **9**
Parr St. *Exe* —5B **4**
Parsonage Way. *Wood* —5G **19**
Parson Clo. *Exm* —5E **21**
Parthia Pl. *Exm* —6G **21**
Partridge Rd. *Exm* —4E **21**
Patricia Clo. *Exe* —2A **4**
Paul St. *Exe* —6H **3** (2B **26**)
Pavilion Pl. *Exe* —1A **10** (3D **26**)
Paynes Ct. *Exe* —4F **5**
Pebble La. *Bud S* —5E **25**
Peel Clo. *Top* —3E **17**
Peep La. *Exe* —6G **3**
Pellinore Rd. *Exe* —3E **5**
Pendle. *Bud S* —5E **25**
Pendragon Rd. *Exe* —2D **4**
Penitentiary Ct. *Exe* —1A **10** (4C **26**)
Penleonard Clo. *Exe* —1C **10**
Pennsylvania Clo. *Exe* —4B **4**
Pennsylvania Cres. *Exe* —4A **4**
Pennsylvania Pk. *Exe* —3B **4**
Pennsylvania Rd. *Exe* —1A **4**
Penny La. *Exmin* —4A **16**
Pentgrove Ct. *Exm* —2F **23**
Perceval Rd. *Exe* —3E **5**
Percy Rd. *Exe* —3H **9**
Perriam's Pl. *Bud S* —4E **25**
Perridge Clo. *Exe* —3E **9**
Perriman's Row. *Exm* —2C **22**
Perrin Way. *Exe* —3H **5**
Perry Rd. *Exe* —4H **3**
Perth Clo. *Exe* —2C **4**
Peryam Cres. *Exe* —2E **11**
Peterborough Rd. *Exe* —5E **3**
Phear Av. *Exm* —2D **22**
Philip Rd. *Exe* —4D **4**
Phillips Av. *Exm* —6D **20**
Pickwick Arc. *Exe* —3B **26**
Pier Head. *Exm* —3A **22**
Pilton La. *Exe* —4H **5**
Pinbrook M. *Pin* —2G **5**
Pinbrook Rd. *Pin* —3H **5**
Pinces Cotts. *Exe* —3G **9**
Pinces Gdns. *Exe* —3G **9**
Pinces Rd. *Exe* —3G **9**
Pine Av. *Exe* —5F **3**
Pineridge Clo. *Exe* —2F **9**
Pines Rd. *Exm* —4E **21**
Pinhoe Rd. *Whip* —5C **4**
Pinhoe Trad. Est. *Exe* —3H **5**
Pinncourt La. *Exe* —2B **6**
Pinn Hill. *Exe* —2B **6**
Pinn La. *Exe* —3A **6**
Pinn Valley Rd. *Exe* —3B **6**
Pinwood La. *Exe* —2F **5**
Pinwood Mdw. Dri. *Exe* —2F **5**
Pippin Clo. *Exe* —6G **5**
Plassey Clo. *Exe* —2B **4**
Playmoor Dri. *Exe* —3A **6**
Plaza, The. *Exe* —2H **9** (5A **26**)
Plumtree Dri. *Exe* —2F **11**
Point Ter. *Exm* —3A **22**
Polehouse La. *Ide* —6E **9**
Politimore Sq. *Exe* —5A **4**
Polsloe Rd. *Exe* —5C **4**
Poplar Clo. *Exe* —3G **9**
Poplar Clo. *Exm* —4F **21**
Poplar Row. *Bud S* —5F **25**
Poplars, The. *Exe* —2A **6**
Poppy Clo. *Exe* —4D **2**
Portland Av. *Exm* —3D **22**
Portland St. *Exe* —6C **4**
Portmer Clo. *Exm* —4G **21**
Post Office St. *Exe* —6A **4** (2D **26**)
Pottles Clo. *Exmin* —5A **16**
Pound Clo. *Top* —2E **17**
Pound La. *Exm* —5D **20**
Pound La. *Top* —2E **17**
Pound La. *Wood* —5G **19**
Pound La. Trad. Est. *Exm* —6E **21**
Pound St. *Exm* —3C **22**
Powderham Clo. *Top* —2E **17**
Powderham Cres. *Exe* —4B **4**
Powderham Rd. *Exe* —2G **9**
Premier Pl. *Exe* —1B **10**
Prescot Rd. *Exe* —1E **9**
Preston St. *Exe* —1H **9** (4B **26**)
Pretoria Rd. *Exe* —5D **4**
Priddis Clo. *Exm* —4E **21**
Pridhams Way. *Exmin* —4A **16**
Priestley Av. *Exe* —4F **5**
Primrose Lawn. *Exe* —4D **2**
Prince Charles Clo. *Exm* —6G **21**
Prince Charles Rd. *Exe* —4C **4**
Prince of Wales Dri. *Exm* —1F **23**
Prince of Wales Rd. *Exe* —4H **3**
Princesshay. *Exe* —6A **4** (2C **26**)
Prince's Sq. *Exe* —2G **9** (6A **26**)
Princes St. *Exm* —3C **22**
Prince's St. E. *Exe* —3G **9** (6A **26**)
Prince's St. N. *Exe* —2G **9**
Prince's St. S. *Exe* —3G **9**
Prince's St. W. *Exe* —3G **9**
Priory Rd. *Exe* —4C **4**
Prison La. *Exe* —5A **4**
Prospect Gdns. *Exe* —5C **4**
Prospect Pk. *Exe* —4B **4**
Prospect Pl. *Exe* —2G **9**
Puckridge Rd. *Exe* —2H **5**
Puffin Way. *Exe* —3D **8**
Pulling Rd. *Exe* —2H **5**
Pulpit Wlk. *Exe* —1E **15**
Purcell Clo. *Exe* —1G **11**
Pynes Hill. *Ryd L* —4G **11**
Pytes Gdns. *Cly G* —1A **18**

Quadrant, The. *Exe* —1B **10**
Quarries, The. *Exe* —2D **8**
Quarry La. *Exe* —1F **11**
Quarry Pk. Rd. *Exe* —2G **11**
Quay Bri. *Exe* —1H **9** (4B **26**)
Quay Hill. *Exe* —1H **9** (4B **26**)
Quay House Visitor Centre. —1A **10** (4C **26**)
Quay La. *Exe* —1A **10** (4C **26**)
Quay Steps. *Exe* —4C **26**
Quay, The. *Exe* —1A **10** (4C **26**)
*Queen's Ct. Exm —3C **22***
(off Queen St.)
Queen's Cres. *Exe* —5A **4**
Queen's Dri. *Exm* —4D **22**
Queens Dri., The. *Exe* —4H **3**
Queensland Dri. *Exe* —2C **4**
Queen's Rd. *Bud S* —3D **24**
Queen's Rd. *Exe* —3G **9** (6A **26**)
Queen's Ter. *Exe* —5H **3**
Queen St. *Bud S* —5E **25**
Queen St. *Exe* —5H **3** (1B **26**)
Queen St. *Exm* —3C **22**
Quintet Clo. *Exe* —1G **11**

Rackclose La. *Exe* —1H **9** (3A **26**)
Rackfield Cotts. *Exe* —4F **3**
Rack St. *Exe* —1H **9** (3B **26**)
Raddenstile Ct. *Exm* —3D **22**

Raddenstile La. *Exm* —3D **22**
Radford Rd. *Exe* —1A **10** (4D **26**)
Radnor Pl. *Exe* —1B **10**
Ragg La. *Bud S* —5E **25**
Raglans. *Exe* —6A **10**
Railway Cotts. *Exe* —6G **5**
Raleigh Ct. *Bud S* —3F **25**
Raleigh Rd. *Bud S* —4F **25**
Raleigh Rd. *Exe* —1B **10**
Randell's Grn. *Exm* —3G **23**
Raven Clo. *Exe* —3A **4**
Rayleigh Rd. *Exm* —3C **22**
Rayners. *Kennf* —6C **14**
Read Clo. *Exm* —6E **21**
Rectory Dri. *Alp* —6H **9**
Rectory Gdns. *Cly G* —2A **18**
Redcliff Ct. *Bud S* —5E **25**
Red Cow Village. *Exe* —4G **3**
Reddaway Dri. *Exmin* —3H **15**
Redhills. *Bud S* —5E **25**
Redhills. *Exe* —1F **9**
Redhills Clo. *Exe* —6E **3**
Redlands Clo. *Exe* —4E **5**
Red Lion La. *Exe* —5B **4**
Redvers Rd. *Exe* —1G **9**
Redwood Clo. *Exm* —4F **21**
Regency Cres. *Exm* —3E **23**
Regent's Pk. *Exe* —6C **4**
(in two parts)
Regent Sq. *Hea* —1D **10**
Rennes Dri. *Exe* —3A **4**
Renslade Ho. *Exe* —4A **26**
Retail Pk. Clo. *Exe* —3H **9**
Retreat Dri., The. *Top* —2D **16**
Retreat Rd. *Top* —3E **17**
Rews Mdw. *Exe* —3B **6**
Rews Pk. Dri. *Exe* —3B **6**
Rexona Clo. *Exe* —4G **9**
Reynolds Ct. *Exe* —3H **5**
Ribston Av. *Exe* —6G **5**
Ribston Clo. *Exe* —6G **5**
Rices M. *Exe* —3G **9**
Richard Clo. *Exm* —5F **21**
Richmond Rd. *Exe* —6H **3** (1A **26**)
Richmond Rd. *Exm* —2F **23**
Ridgeway. *Exe* —1G **3**
Rifford Rd. *Exe* —2E **11**
Ringswell Av. *Exe* —6G **5**
Ringswell Pk. *Exe* —1G **11**
Ripon Clo. *Exe* —6E **3**
River Front. *Ext* —6H **17**
Rivermead Av. *Exm* —5C **20**
Rivermead Rd. *Exe* —3B **10**
Riverside Ct. *Exe* —4C **26**
Riverside Rd. *Top* —2E **17**
Riversmeet. *Top* —5G **17**
Rivers Wlk. *Exe* —1C **16**
Riverview. *Exmin* —5B **16**
Riverview Dri. *Exe* —4F **3**
Riviera Ter. *Exmin* —5B **16**
Roberts Rd. *Exe* —1A **10** (4D **26**)
Roche Gdns. *Exe* —6E **11**
Rockside. *Exe* —6G **3**
Rockside Vs. *Exe* —6G **3**
Rodney Clo. *Exm* —2H **23**
Rolle Cotts. *Bud S* —3B **24**
Rolle Rd. *Bud S* —5E **25**
Rolle Rd. *Exm* —3C **22**
Rollestone Cres. *Exe* —2C **4**
Rolle St. *Exm* —3C **22**
Rolle, The. *Bud S* —5E **25**
Rolle Vs. *Exm* —3C **22**
Roly Poly Hill. *Exe* —4E **9**
Romsey Dri. *Exe* —1C **10**
Rosebank Cres. *Exe* —3B **4**
Rosebarn Av. *Exe* —3B **4**
Rosebarn La. *Exe* —2B **4**
Rosebery Rd. *Exe* —4C **4**
Rosebery Rd. *Exm* —1C **22**
Roseland Av. *Exe* —6E **5**
Roseland Cres. *Exe* —6E **5**
Roseland Dri. *Exe* —1E **11**
Rosemary St. *Exe* —1F **9**
Rosemont Ct. *Exe* —5H **9**
Roseway. *Exm* —1H **23**
Rosewood Cres. *Cly M* —4G **13**
Rosewood Ter. *Exe* —4B **4**
Ross Clo. *Exe* —3B **6**
Rougemont Castle. —6A **4** (4C **26**)
Rougemont Ct. *Exmin* —4H **15**
Roundhill Clo. *Exe* —1G **3**
Roundhouse La. *Exm* —5D **20**
Round Table Meet. *Exe* —3E **5**
Rowan Cft. *Exe* —6D **4**
Rowan Way. *Exe* —5F **3**
Rowhorne Rd. *Nadd* —2A **2**
Rowlstone Clo. *Exm* —4E **21**
Royal Albert Memorial Museum & Art Gallery. —6H **3** (1B **26**)
Royal Av., The. *Exm* —2B **22**
Royal Clo. *Exe* —1D **14**
Royston Ct. *Exe* —4G **5**
Rugby Rd. *Exe* —2G **9**
Rushforth Pl. *Exe* —4E **3**
Russell St. *Exe* —6B **4**
Russell Ter. *Exe* —6H **3** (1A **26**)
Russell Way. *Exe* —3G **11**
Russet Av. *Exe* —6G **5**
Russet Clo. *Exe* —6G **5**
Rutherford St. *Exe* —2E **11**
Rydon La. *Exe* —5F **11**
Rydon La. *Ext* —6B **18**
Rydon Pk. Cvn. Pk. *Ryd L* —2H **11**
Ryll Clo. *Exm* —2D **22**
Ryll Ct. Dri. *Exm* —2D **22**
Ryll Gro. *Exm* —2D **22**
Ryll La. *Bud S* —5F **25**

Sadler Clo. *Exm* —1G **23**
St Albans Clo. *Exe* —6E **3**
St Andrew's Rd. *Exe* —1E **3**
St Andrew's Rd. *Exm* —3B **22**
St Annes Rd. *Exe* —5C **4**
St Bernards Clo. *Exe* —2B **10**
St Clememts La. *Exe* —5G **3**
St Davids Hill. *Exe* —5G **3** (1A **26**)
St Davids Ter. *Exe* —6H **3** (1A **26**)
St Georges Hall & Market. —6A **3** (3B **26**)
St George's Ter. *Shi S* —4A **14**
St German's Rd. *Exe* —4A **4**
St Hill Clo. *Exe* —4G **9**
St Ida's Clo. *Ide* —5D **8**
St James' Clo. *Exe* —5B **4**
St James' Rd. *Exe* —5B **4**
St James' Ter. *Exe* —5B **4**
St John's Rd. *Exe* —5C **4**
St John's Rd. *Exm* —6F **21**
St Johns Vs. *Exe* —1D **10**
St Katherine's Rd. *Exe* —4E **5**
St Lawrence Cres. *Exe* —6H **5**
St Leonard's Av. *Exe* —2A **10** (5D **26**)
St Leonards Pl. *Cly M* —3C **12**
St Leonard's Pl. *Exe* —1B **10**
St Leonard's Rd. *Exe* —2B **10**
St Loves Ter. *Exe* —2E **11**
St Loyes Rd. *Exe* —1E **11**
St Margaret's Vw. *Exm* —2H **23**
St Mark's Av. *Exe* —5D **4**
St Mary's Arches. *Exe* —6H **3** (2B **26**)
St Mary's Steps Ter. *Exe* —3B **26**
St Matthews Clo. *Exe* —6B **4**
St Michaels Clo. *Cly H* —4F **7**
St Michaels Clo. *Exe* —5H **9**
St Michaels Hill. *Cly H* —4F **7**
St Michael's M. *Exe* —1A **26**
St Nicholas Priory. —3A **26**
St Olaves Clo. *Exe* —1H **9** (3B **26**)
St Peter's Cathedral. —6A **4** (2C **26**)
St Peter's Mt. *Exe* —6D **2**
St Petrocks Clo. *Exe* —1B **10**
St Sevan Way. *Exm* —4G **21**
St Sidewells Av. *Exe* —5A **4**
St Thomas Cen. *Exe* —2G **9**
St Thomas M. *Exe* —2G **9**
Salem Pl. *Exe* —5B **4**
Salisbury Rd. *Exe* —4C **4**
Salisbury Rd. *Exm* —2C **22**
Salter's Ct. *Exe* —2E **11**
Salter's Rd. *Exe* —2E **11**
Salterton Rd. *Exm* —3D **22**
(in two parts)
Salting Hill. *Bud S* —5G **25**
Salutary Mt. *Hea* —1D **10**
Sampson's Hill. *Shi S* —4B **14**
Sampsons La. *Exe* —5C **4**
Sanders Rd. *Exe* —3H **5**
Sandfords. *Kennf* —6D **14**
Sandford Wlk. *Exe* —6B **4**
Sandpiper Ct. *Exe* —3H **5**
Sandpiper Dri. *Ext* —6A **18**
Sandpiper Grn. *Exe* —2D **8**
Sannerville Way. *Exmin* —2A **16**
Sargent Clo. *Exe* —6G **5**
Sarlsdown Rd. *Exm* —2F **23**
Saville Rd. *Exe* —1F **9**
Savoy Hill. *Exe* —2E **5**
Saxon Av. *Exe* —2A **6**
Saxon Rd. *Exe* —6D **4**
Scarsdale. *Exm* —4E **23**
School Hill. *Lymp* —2A **20**
School La. *Exe* —5E **11**
School La. *Exm* —6D **20**
School Rd. *Exe* —2G **9** (6A **26**)
Schooner's Ct. *Exm* —3A **22**
Scott Av. *Exe* —3D **10**
Scott Dri. *Exm* —5D **20**
Scratch Face La. *Exe* —4B **8**
Seabrook Av. *Exe* —1C **16**
Seafield Av. *Exm* —5C **20**
Second Av. *Exe* —6D **4**
(EX1)
Second Av. *Exe* —1C **16**
(EX2)
Sedgeclaire Clo. *Exe* —3B **6**
*Senate Ct. Exm —6G **21***
(off Senate Way)
Senate Way. *Exm* —6F **21**
Sentrys Orchard. *Exmin* —5B **16**
Serge Ct. *Exe* —1H **9** (4B **26**)
Setting Sail Exhibition. —2A **10** (5C **26**)
Seymour Ct. *Exm* —5D **20**
Seymour Rd. *Exm* —5D **20**
Shackleton Clo. *Exm* —5D **20**
Shaftesbury Rd. *Exe* —2G **9**
Shakespeare Rd. *Exe* —3D **10**
Shakespeare Way. *Exm* —3E **21**
Sharpes Ct. *Exm* —3A **22**
Shearman Ct. *Exe* —1H **9** (4B **26**)
Shelley Clo. *Exe* —4G **9**
Shelley Ct. *Exm* —3A **22**
Shelly Rd. *Exm* —3A **22**
(in two parts)
Shelton Pl. *Hea* —6D **4**
Sheppard Rd. *Exe* —2B **4**
Sheppards Row. *Exm* —2C **22**
Sherbrook Clo. *Bud S* —5D **24**
Sherbrook Hill. *Bud S* —5D **24**
Shercroft Clo. *Broad* —2G **7**
Sheridan Rd. *Exe* —4G **5**
Sherwood Clo. *Exe* —1D **10**
Sherwood Dri. *Exm* —4F **21**
Shillingford La. *Kennf* —4C **14**
Shillingford Rd. *Exe* —1C **14**
Ship La. *Cly H* —4F **7**
Shirley Clo. *Exm* —3F **21**
Shortwood Clo. *Bud S* —3D **24**
Shortwood La. *Bud S* —1B **24**
Shrubbery, The. *Top* —3F **17**
*Shute Mdw. St. Exm —2C **22***
(off Meadow St.)
Sidmouth Rd. *Exe* —1G **11**
Sidwell St. *Exe* —6A **4** (1D **26**)
Silverbirch Clo. *Exe* —3E **11**
Silverdale. *Exm* —4G **21**
Silver La. *Exe* —5B **4**
Silver Ter. *Exe* —5G **3** (1A **26**)
Silverton Rd. *Mar B* —6B **10**
Simey Clo. *Exe* —5F **3**
Sir Alex Wlk. *Top* —2D **16**
Sivell Pl. *Exe* —1D **10**
*Sleepy Hollow. Exe —1C **16***
(off Newport Pk.)
Smithfield Rd. *Exe* —6G **9**
Smythen St. *Exe* —1H **9** (3B **26**)
Solar Cres. *Exe* —2F **9**
Somerset Av. *Exe* —2E **9**

Somerville Clo. *Exm* —6F **21**
South Av. *Exe* —6C **4**
Southbrook Rd. *Exe* —4E **11**
Southernhay E. *Exe* —1A **10** (3C **26**)
Southernhay Gdns. *Exe* —6A **4** (2D **26**)
Southernhay W. *Exe* —1A **10** (3D **26**)
Southern Rd. *Exm* —1C **22**
Southern Wood. *Exm* —5G **21**
S. Farm Rd. *Bud S* —3F **25**
South Ga. *Exe* —1A **10** (4C **26**)
S. Grange. *Exe* —3H **11**
Southlands. *Exe* —6C **4**
S. Lawn Ter. *Exe* —6D **4**
S. Parade. *Bud S* —5F **25**
Southport Av. *Exe* —1E **9**
South St. *Exe* —6H **3** (4B **26**)
South St. *Exm* —3C **22**
S. View Ter. *Exe* —4B **4**
S. View Ter. *Exmin* —4B **16**
Sovereign Clo. *Exm* —6G **21**
Sowden La. *Lymp* —3A **20**
Sowton Ind. Est. *Sow I* —1A **12** (in two parts)
Sowton La. *Sow* —5C **6**
Spacex Gallery. —3B **26**
Spencer Clo. *Exm* —5G **21**
Spenser Av. *Exe* —3D **10**
Spicer Rd. *Exe* —1B **10**
Spicer Rd. E. *Exe* —1B **10**
Spider's La. *Exm* —4E **21** (in two parts)
Spinney Clo. *Exe* —2G **11**
Springfield Rd. *Exe* —4B **4**
Springfield Rd. *Exm* —6D **20**
Spring Path. *Exe* —5B **4**
Spruce Clo. *Exe* —2F **5**
Spruce Clo. *Exm* —4F **21**
Spurway Hill. *Exmin* —5H **15**
Square, The. *Exe* —4F **3**
Staddon Clo. *Exe* —5F **5**
Stafford Rd. *Exe* —1F **9**
Stanford Rd. *Exe* —1G **11**
Stanley M. *Bud S* —4E **25**
Stanley Sq. *Top* —4F **17**
Stanley Way. *Exm* —3F **21**
Stanwey. *Exe* —1E **11**
*Staple's Bldgs. Exm —2C **22** (off Parade)*
*Staples M. Exm —2C **22** (off Exeter Rd.)*
Star Barton La. *White* —1B **2**
Station Rd. *Broad* —1F **7**
Station Rd. *Bud S* —4E **25**
Station Rd. *Exmin* —5C **16** (in two parts)
Station Rd. *Ext* —6A **18**
Station Rd. *Exw* —4F **3**
Station Rd. *Ide* —5C **8**
Station Rd. *Pin* —3A **6**
Station Rd. *Top* —3F **17**
Station Yd. *Exe* —6H **3** (1A **26**)
Steeple Dri. *Exe* —1D **14**
Stepcote Hill. *Exe* —1H **9** (3B **26**)
Steps Clo. *Exe* —3B **6**
Stevenstone Rd. *Exm* —2F **23**
Stewart Clo. *Exm* —1G **23**
Stocker Rd. *Exe* —3H **3**
Stoke Hill. *Exe* —3C **4**
Stoke Hill Cres. *Exe* —3C **4**
Stokelyne. *Exm* —6E **21**
Stoke Mdw. Clo. *Exe* —2C **4**
Stoke Rd. *Exe* —1F **3**
Stoke Valley Rd. *Exe* —1B **4**
Stoneborough Ct. *Bud S* —4F **25**
Stoneborough La. *Bud S* —4F **25**
Stone La. *Exe* —3G **9**
Stone La. Retail Pk. *Mar B* —3H **9**
Stoneyford Pk. *Bud S* —4F **25**
Stoney La. *Wood S* —2G **19**
Stover Ct. *Exe* —5B **4**
Strand. *Exm* —3C **22**
Strand. *Top* —4F **17**
Strand Ct. *Top* —4F **17**
Strand, The. *Lymp* —2A **20**
Strand Vw. *Top* —4F **17**
Stratford Av. *Exe* —4G **5**
Strawberry Av. *Exe* —6A **10**
Strawberry Hill. *Lymp* —2A **20**
Streatham Dri. *Exe* —4G **3**
Streatham Ri. *Exe* —4G **3**
Struges Rd. *Exm* —1F **23**
Stuart Rd. *Exe* —6D **4**
Sullivan Rd. *Exe* —1G **11**
Summer Clo. *Exe* —4F **5**
Summer Clo. *Exm* —1G **23**
Summerfield. *Wood* —4G **19**
Summerlands St. *Exe* —5B **4**
Summer La. *Exe* —3F **5**
Summer La. *Exm* —4C **20**
Summerway *Exe* —4F **5**
Sunhill Av. *Top* —2F **17**
Sunhill La. *Top* —2F **17**
Sunnymoor Clo. *Exe* —3B **6**
Sunwine Pl. *Exm* —3D **22**
Surbiton Cres. *Exe* —2F **9**
Sussex Clo. *Exe* —2E **9**
Swains Ct. *Top* —3E **17**
Swains Rd. *Bud S* —3F **25**
Swallow Dri. *Exe* —3D **8**
Swallowfield Rd. *Exe* —4E **11**
Swan Yd. *Exe* —1G **9**
Sweetbrier La. *Exe* —6E **5**
Swiss Clo. *Exm* —4D **20**
Sycamore Clo. *Exe* —1F **11**
Sycamore Clo. *Exm* —5G **21**
Sydney Rd. *Exe* —2G **9** (6A **26**)
Sylvan Av. *Exe* —3B **4**
Sylvan Clo. *Exm* —5C **20**
Sylvania Dri. *Exe* —2C **4**
Sylvan Rd. *Exe* —3B **4**

Taddiforde Rd. *Exe* —5G **3**
Taddyforde Ct. *Exe* —4G **3**
Taddyforde Ct. Mans. *Exe* —4G **3**
Taddyforde Est. *Exe* —4G **3**
Tamarisk Clo. *Exe* —2F **5**
Tan La. *Exe* —3H **9** (6B **26**)
Tappers Clo. *Top* —3F **17**
Tarbet Av. *Exe* —5D **4**
Taunton Clo. *Exe* —3G **9**
Tavistock Rd. *Exe* —5G **3**
Teazle Ct. *Exe* —1H **9** (4B **26**)
Tedburn Rd. *White* —6A **2**
Tedstone La. *Lymp* —1C **20**
Telford Rd. *Exe* —5G **3**
Temple Rd. *Exe* —1A **10** (4D **26**)
Tennyson Av. *Exe* —3D **10**
Tennyson Way. *Exm* —4E **21**
Thackeray Rd. *Exe* —4G **5**
Third Av. *Exe* —6D **4** (nr. First Av.)
Third Av. *Exe* —1C **16** (nr. Moonridge)
Third Av. *Exe* —1H **11** (nr. Nelson Way)
Thomas Clo. *Exm* —3E **21**
Thomas Ct. *Exm* —3C **22**
Thompson Rd. *Exe* —5E **5**
Thornberry Clo. *Exe* —6F **5**
Thorn Clo. *Exe* —6F **5**
Thorndale Ct. *Exe* —4D **2**
Thornfield Clo. *Exm* —5C **20**
Thornlea. *Exe* —5H **3**
Thornpark Ri. *Exe* —6F **5**
Thornton Clo. *Bud S* —5E **25**
Thornton Hill. *Exe* —4A **4**
Thorpe Av. *Exm* —4D **20**
Threecorner Pl. *Exe* —6A **10**
Thurlow Rd. *Exe* —4C **4**
Tidwell Clo. *Bud S* —3E **25**
Tidwell La. *Bud S* —1E **25**
Tidwell Rd. *Bud S* —3E **25**
*Tin La. Exe —2G **9** (off Churchfield Path)*
Tintagel Clo. *Exe* —2E **5**
Tithebarn Copse. *Exe* —4B **6**
Tithebarn La. *Exe* —4B **6**
Tollards Rd. *Exe* —5E **11**
Topsham Museum. —4F **17**
Topsham Rd. *Exe* —2B **10** (5D **26**)
Tor Clo. *Exe* —3E **5**
Toronto Ho. *Exe* —4C **4**
Toronto Rd. *Exe* —5B **4**
Tottons Ct. *Exe* —6G **9**
Towerfield. *Top* —1E **17**
Tower St. *Exm* —3C **22**
Tower Wlk. *Exe* —6A **10**
Townfield. *Exmin* —4A **16**
Towsington La. *Exmin* —6H **15**
Trafalgar Pl. *Exe* —5B **4**
Trafalgar Rd. *Lymp* —1A **20**
Trafford M. *Exe* —3G **11**
Travershes Clo. *Exm* —6D **20**
Trefusis Pl. *Exm* —4C **22**
Trefusis Ter. *Exm* —4C **22**
Tremford Ct. *Bud S* —4D **24**
Trentbridge Sq. *Exe* —2G **11**
Trent M. *Exm* —1G **23**
Tresillian Cotts. *Top* —5F **17**
Tresillian Gdns. *Exe* —4C **4**
Tresillian Gdns. *Top* —4F **17**
Trevena. *Cly M* —3C **12**
Trews Weir Reach. *Exe* —2B **10**
Trigg M. *Top* —2E **17**
Trinfield Av. *Exm* —6D **20**
Trinity Ct. *Exe* —1A **10** (3D **26**)
Trinity Rd. *Exm* —3A **22**
Tristan Clo. *Exe* —2E **5**
Trood La. *Matf* —2F **15**
Truro Dri. *Exe* —5E **3**
Truro Dri. *Exm* —3F **21**
Trusham Rd. *Mar B* —4A **10**
Tuckers Hall. —1H **9** (3A **26**)
Tuckfield Clo. *Exe* —2E **11**
Tudor Ct. *Exe* —1H **9** (3A **26**)
Tudor St. *Exe* —1H **9** (3A **26**)
Tuffrey Clo. *Exe* —4D **4**
Tugela Ter. *Cly M* —3C **12**
Turnbull Cres. *Wood* —6G **19**
Turner Av. *Exm* —2D **22**
Two Acre Ct. *Exe* —6G **9**
Two Stone La. *Kennf* —6A **14**

Underground Passages. —4C **26**
Underhill. *Lymp* —3A **20**
Underhill Cres. *Lymp* —3A **20**
Underhill Ter. *Top* —3F **17**
Union Rd. *Exe* —4B **4**
Union St. *Exe* —2G **9** (5A **26**)
Union St. *Exm* —3C **22**
Uplands Dri. *Exe* —3E **5**
Up. Church St. *Exm* —3C **22**
Up. Paul St. *Exe* —6H **3** (1B **26**)
Up. Stoneborough La. *Bud S* —4E **25**
Up. West Ter. *Bud S* —4E **25**

Vachell Cres. *Exe* —1H **11**
Vale Rd. *Exm* —2F **23**
Vales Rd. *Bud S* —4F **25**
Valley Pk. Clo. *Exe* —2B **4**
Valley Rd. *Cly M* —3F **13**
Valley Rd. *Exe* —5F **3**
Valley Way. *Exm* —4G **21**
Vansittart Dri. *Exm* —4E **21**
Varco Sq. *Exe* —2G **11**
Vaughan Ri. *Exe* —6F **5**
Vaughan Rd. *Exe* —6F **5**
Veitch Gdns. *Exe* —1D **14**
Velwell Rd. *Exe* —5H **3**
Venny Bri. *Exe* —3H **5**
Verney St. *Exe* —5B **4**
Vernon Rd. *Exm* —5F **21**
Vestry Dri. *Exe* —6H **9**
Vicarage Gdns. *Exe* —2G **9**
Vicarage La. *Pin* —2A **6**
Victor Clo. *Exe* —1E **11**
Victoria Pk. Rd. *Exe* —2C **10**
Victoria Pl. *Bud S* —5E **25**
Victoria Pl. *Exm* —3C **22**
Victoria Rd. *Exe* —4B **4**
Victoria Rd. *Exm* —3B **22**
Victoria Rd. *Top* —3F **17**
Victoria St. *Exe* —4B **4**
Victoria Way. *Exm* —3B **22**
Victoria Yd. *Exe* —6H **3** (1B **26**)
Victor La. *Exe* —1E **11**
Victor St. *Exe* —1E **11**
Village Clo. *Exm* —2H **23**
Village Rd. *Wood S* —1G **19**
Village, The. *Cly M* —3C **12**
Vine Clo. *Exe* —1B **10**

Vine Ho. *Bud S* —4F **25**
Vision Hill Rd. *Bud S* —3F **25**
Vuefield Hill. *Exe* —3E **9**

Wagoners Way. *Exe* —4G **3**
Wallace Av. *Exe* —4F **5**
Wallclose La. *Bud S* —3H **25**
Walls Clo. *Exm* —5F **21**
Walnut Clo. *Exmin* —4A **16**
Walnut Gdns. *Exe* —5G **3**
Walnut Gro. *Exm* —2E **23**
Walnut Rd. *Exe* —4D **10**
Walpole Clo. *Exe* —3G **5**
Walton Rd. *Exe* —1G **11**
Wardrew Rd. *Exe* —1F **9**
Warneford Gdns. *Exm* —5G **21**
Warren Dri. *Bud S* —3F **25**
Warren La. *Exe* —5A **4**
Warwick Av. *Exe* —1G **11**
Warwick Rd. *Exe* —6G **5**
Warwick Way. *Exe* —4G **5**
Waterbeer St. *Exe* —6H **3** (2B **26**)
Watergate. *Exe* —1A **10** (4C **26**)
Water La. *Exe* —2H **9** (5B **26**)
Waterloo Rd. *Exe* —3G **9**
Waterside. *Exe* —2H **9** (5B **26**)
Waterslade La. *Cly H* —4G **7**
Watery La. *Bud* —4F **19**
Waverley Av. *Exe* —5A **4**
Waverley Rd. *Exm* —1C **22**
Waybrook Cotts. *Alp* —1D **14**
Waybrook Cres. *Exe* —6H **9**
Waybrook La. *Shi A* —2C **14**
Wayland Av. *Exe* —2B **10**
Wayside Cres. *Exe* —5F **5**
Wear Barton Rd. *Exe* —6F **11**
Wear Clo. *Exe* —1C **16**
Weavers Ct. *Exe* —4B **26**
Webber's Farm Cvn. Pk. *Wood* —5H **19**
Webley Rd. *Exe* —3F **9**
Weirfield Path. *Exe* —3B **10**
Weirfield Rd. *Exe* —2A **10** (5D **26**)
Welcombe St. *Exe* —2H **9** (6B **26**)
Wellington Clo. *Exe* —1H **11**
Wellington Rd. *Exe* —3G **9**
Wellpark Clo. *Exe* —1F **9**
Wells Clo. *Exm* —3G **21**
Well St. *Exe* —5B **4**
Wellswood Gdns. *Exe* —1E **9**
Wendover Way. *Exe* —4F **11**
Wentworth Gdns. *Exe* —2E **9**
Wesley Clo. *Exe* —3G **9**
Wesley Way. *Exe* —6H **9**
Wessex Clo. *Top* —2D **16**
Wessex Est. *Exe* —4G **3**
West Av. *Exe* —4A **4**
Westbourne Ter. *Bud S* —5D **24**
Westbrook Clo. *Exe* —4F **5**
Westcombe. *Alp* —6H **9**
W. Down La. *Exm* —2H **23**
Western Av. *Exe* —1D **16**
Western Rd. *Exe* —1G **9**
Western Way. *Exe* —1H **9** (in two parts)
Westfield. *Exmin* —5B **16**
Westfield Clo. *Bud S* —4E **25**
Westfield Rd. *Bud S* —4E **25**
W. Garth Rd. *Exe* —2G **3**
W. Grove Rd. *Exe* —1B **10**
W. Hill. *Bud S* —4D **24**
W. Hill Ct. *Bud S* —5D **24**
W. Hill Gdns. *Bud S* —5D **24**
W. Hill La. *Bud S* —4D **24**
Westlands. *Exm* —3E **23**
Westminster Clo. *Exm* —4F **21**
Westminster Rd. *Exe* —6D **2**
Westown Rd. *Exe* —5B **8** (in two parts)
Westpoint. (Devon County Showground) —3F **13**
West St. *Exe* —1H **9** (3A **26**)
West Ter. *Bud S* —4E **25**
West Ter. *Exe* —6D **4**
W. View Ter. *Exe* —1H **9** (3A **26**)
Westward Dri. *Exm* —2D **22**
Westwood La. *Long* —2A **8**
Weycroft Clo. *Exe* —6H **5**
Wheatley Clo. *Exe* —1E **9**
Wheatley Ct. *Exe* —3B **26**
Wheatsheaf Way. *Exe* —5G **9**
Whiddon La. *Ide* —6B **8**
Whipton Barton Rd. *Exe* —5F **5**
Whipton La. *Exe* —1E **11**
Whipton Rd. *Exe* —4E **5**
Whipton Village Rd. *Exe* —4F **5**
Whitchurch Av. *Exe* —2F **11**
Whitebeam Clo. *Exe* —2F **5**
White Cross Rd. *Wood S* —2H **19**
Whitehill La. *Top* —6A **12**
White Lodge. Bud S —5F ***25*** *(off Coastguard Rd.)*
Whiteside Clo. *Exe* —2G **11**
Whitestones. *Exm* —3E **23**
White St. *Top* —4F **17**
Whitethorn Pk. *Exe* —1A **4**
Whiteway Dri. *Exe* —6F **5**
Whitman Clo. *Exm* —3E **21**
Whitycombe Way. *Exe* —4D **2**
Widecombe Way. *Exe* —3C **4**
Widgery Rd. *Exe* —4E **5**
Wilcocks Rd. *Exe* —3H **5**
Wilford Rd. *Exe* —1F **11**
Willey's Av. *Exe* —2H **9** (6A **26**)
Williams Av. *Exe* —2H **9** (5A **26**)
Willoughby Clo. *Exm* —4E **21**
Willow Av. *Exm* —4D **20**
Willow Ct. *Exe* —2E **11**
Willows, The. *Shi S* —4A **14**
Willow Wlk. *Exe* —4B **4**
Willsdown Rd. *Exe* —6A **10**
Wilmot Clo. *Exm* —6G **21**
Wilton Way. *Exe* —6H **5**
Wiltshire Clo. *Exe* —2E **9**
Winchester Av. *Exe* —5E **3**
Winchester Dri. *Exm* —3F **21**
Windermere Clo. *Exe* —6F **3**
Windsor Clo. *Exe* —5G **3**
Windsor Ct. *Exe* —6A **10**
Windsor Sq. *Exm* —2C **22**
Winkleigh Clo. *Exe* —4G **9**
Winslade Pk. Av. *Cly M* —4C **12**
Winston Rd. *Exm* —4G **21**
Wish Mdw. La. *Broad* —1F **7**
Withycombe Pk. Dri. *Exm* —5G **21**
Withycombe Rd. *Exm* —1C **22**
Withycombe Village Rd. *Exm* —1D **22**
Wonford Rd. *Exe* —1B **10**
Wonford St. *Exe* —2E **11**
Woodah Rd. *Exe* —1F **9**
Woodbine Ter. *Exe* —5H **3**
Woodbury Ct. *Exm* —3E **23**
Woodbury Rd. *Cly G* —1A **18**
Woodbury Vw. *Exe* —4G **9**
Woodfield Clo. *Exm* —5G **21**
Woodland Rd. *Exe* —5H **5**
Woodlands. *Bud S* —5C **24**
Woodlands Ct. *Exm* —4D **20**
Woodlands Dri. *Exm* —4D **20**
Woodlands Way. *Cly M* —3F **13**
Wood La. *Exm* —6F **21**
Woodleigh Clo. *Exe* —1G **3**
Woodstock Rd. *Exe* —1E **11**
Woodville Rd. *Exe* —3H **9**
Woodville Rd. *Exm* —1C **22**
Woodwater Cotts. *Exe* —3G **11**
Woodwater La. *Exe* —2E **11**
Woolaway Av. *Exmin* —4B **16**
Woolsery Av. *Exe* —4F **5**
Woolsery Clo. *Exe* —4F **5**
Woolsery Gro. *Exe* —4E **5**
Wordsworth Clo. *Exm* —4E **21**
Wotton Cotts. *Pin* —2G **5**
Wotton La. *Lymp* —2C **20**
Wreford's Clo. *Exe* —1F **3**
Wreford's Dri. *Exe* —1G **3**
Wreford's La. *Exe* —1G **3**
Wreford's Link. *Exe* —1G **3**
Wrentham Est. *Exe* —4B **4**
Wright's La. *Exm* —1H **21**
Wykes Rd. *Exe* —5D **4**
Wynards La. *Exe* —1A **10** (3D **26**)
Wyndham Av. *Exe* —6D **4**
Wynford Rd. *Exe* —3D **4**

Yeoford Way. *Exe* —6B **10**
Yew Tree Clo. *Exe* —3C **4**
Yew Tree Clo. *Exm* —4E **21**
York Clo. *Exm* —5G **21**
York Rd. *Exe* —5A **4**
York Ter. *Exe* —5B **4**

Zig Zag Path. *Bud S* —5D **24**